Socialism

Socialism

Concepts in the Social Sciences

Series Editor: Frank Parkin
Magdalen College, Oxford

Published Titles

Liberalism	*John Gray*
Ideology	*David McLellan*
Conservatism	*Robert Nisbet*
Race and Ethnicity	*John Rex*
Bureaucracy	*David Beetham*
Socialism	*Bernard Crick*
Democracy	*Anthony Arblaster*
Property	*Alan Ryan*

Forthcoming Titles

Power	*Peter Bachrach*
Utopianism	*Krishan Kumar*
Class	*Steven Lukes*
Gender	*Mary McIntosh*
Status	*Bryan Turner*

Socialism

Bernard Crick

OPEN UNIVERSITY PRESS
Milton Keynes

Open University Press
Open University Educational Enterprises Limited
12 Cofferidge Close
Stony Stratford
Milton Keynes MK11 1BY, England

First published 1987

British Library Cataloguing in Publication Data

Crick, Bernard
    Socialism.——(Concepts in social sciences series).
    1. Socialism
    I. Title   II. Series
    335   HX73

    ISBN 0-335-15388-7
    ISBN 0-335-15387-9 Pbk

Project Management: Clarke Williams

Printed in Great Britain

Contents

Preface and acknowledgements   viii

1   Preconditions   1

2   The Great Revolution   14

3   Early Socialism   28

4   Marx and Marxism:
    Theory and Practice   47

5   An Intermezzo of Texts
    on British Socialism   66

6   The Values
    of Democratic Socialism   78

Bibliography   115
Index   119

Preface and Acknowledgements

For the thinking general reader I have tried to write a short and simple account of a subject which is often needlessly complicated and abstruse. There is something sad and comic in too many books on socialism being almost incomprehensible to anyone except graduates of the Social Sciences. It is more difficult, of course, to try to distil a whole subject to its basic propositions and to uncover its presuppositions than it is to elaborate at great length some special aspect of theory.

One clear fact emerges from trying to get back to beginnings and basics: there is more ground for agreement on the central theoretical beliefs and the main values of democratic Socialism than is often supposed. And there is more common ground too with open-minded, humanistic Marxists; but they, alas, have only recently gained any intellectual ascendancy, and have never had political power anywhere. The other sort have.

Some readers may think that for a short and, I hope, popular book I have given disproportionate space to the origins, even to the pre-history of socialism. This is for two reasons: (i) because its origins are little understood, and unless we have some understanding of the origins and conditions of a doctrine or an institution, we understand very little; (ii) to demonstrate that there was socialism before Marx and that much of it, like Joe Hill, never died and has recently become quite lively again — witness the revival in the British Labour movement of ideas of pluralism, decentralization, suspicion of 'the state' (rather than the old simple eagerness to get hold of it), cooperation and popular liberties. This is not because people have begun reading the pioneers and the forerunners, but because their basic instincts now seem in many respects more correct than those of Engels, of Lenin and of British Fabian 'state socialism'.

But spending space in a small compass on origins, and

viii   *Preface and Acknowledgements*

wanting to leave myself room in the last chapter to establish
just what is the common core of theory and values in British
democratic socialism, I have not given space to the once
familiar tale of its emergence (as can be found most recently
and ably told in Geoffrey Foote's *The Labour Party's Political
Thought: a History* (Croom Helm, 1985)). Rather, I offer
Chapter 5 as a kind of intermezzo, a collage of typical quota-
tions from the British tradition. Let them speak for themselves,
briefly. Antony Wright's *English Socialism* (Longman, 1983)
is a good and far fuller anthology, and his *Socialism: Theory
and Practices* (OUP, 1986) contains his own larger views on
pluralistic socialism. I have gained from reading recently
Michael Rustin's *For Pluralist Socialism* (Verso, 1985) and
also Gavin Kitching's *Rethinking Socialism* (Methuen, 1983).

Democratic socialism in Britain is neither a betrayal nor a
falling off from the one 'true socialism' (there never was such
a thing, except at the point of a gun), nor simply a compromise
practical position; it is at least an equally authentic popular
tradition to Marxism, if certainly more eclectic and less theo-
logical — which in my book are virtues. And some of these
considerations now seem to be impressing themselves on even
the leader of the Soviet Union.

It could help the reader to know that I distinguish more
sharply than is common between 'theory' and 'doctrine'. By a
theory I mean a generalization or a general explanation:
theories are either concerned empirically with what is the case
or with defining a logical explanatory language. By a doctrine
I mean a coherent body of assertions about what ought to be
the case. Socialism, like conservatism and liberalism, is plainly
both a theory and a doctrine. The distinction, indeed, is one of
emphasis, it is not absolute. All social and political theories
make some assumptions about values, and all doctrines claim,
not merely to be right, but to be workable. When I talk of
political 'rhetoric' I mean doctrines being used to persuade,
usually the unconvinced. Aristotle said that the true rheto-
rician must be master of a subject, be able to define the effect
intended and must know well the audience that has to be
convinced. 'Mere rhetoric' is preaching to the converted.

The word 'ideology' is often over-used and can cause difficulties, for it has a wide and wild range of quite different
meanings. For instance 'ideologically correct' used to mean

lies told for the sake of the Communist Party. By 'ideology' some simply mean ideas advanced to persuade. But I find it useful in two different senses: generally to mean a body of ideas that is supposed both to reflect and support a particular social structure or group interest; and, more technically, to mean a body of ideas that claims to offer a total or comprehensive explanation of how societies have developed and will develop. Doctrines are much more specific than 'ideology' in this second and uniquely modern sense: they may claim to deal with the most important things in life, but they don't claim to be about everything; a doctrine relates to things reasonably specific.

The argument about whether socialism is an ideology or a doctrine is logically prior to talking about both what has been meant and what can sensibly be meant by socialism. I do not believe that socialist theory (nor any other) can explain everything, that socialist values are the only values ever to be considered in life, or that whether one is a socialist or not is fully determined by social class. Many things are conditioned, influenced and limited by economic circumstance but nothing is determined. Nonetheless I think I can be more precise than is often believed possible about the common core of meaning in all usages of the concept 'socialism' and the areas in which it is relevant.

Much of this arose in discussions with my last students at Birkbeck College — a truly good and useful place devoted entirely to a sadly restricted number of what each of us should always be, mature part-time students. *I dedicate this book to them* and they alone are entirely to blame if I am not either a more pure or a more fashionably complicated socialist.

Chapter 6 is a shortened version of my *Socialist Values and Time* (Fabian Tract 495), and I thank the Fabian Society for their permission to recycle it.

Bernard Crick
Edinburgh, March 1987

1

Preconditions

Socialism is a product of the modern world. It has no precedent in the ancient or the medieval worlds but they do contain preconditions. From the beginning of written records we find evidence of revolts of the poor against the rich, of oppressed peoples against ruling elites, and of dreams of a perfectly just and usually egalitarian human order. Sometimes these are pictured as acts of human will and reason, sometimes as part of the wrath of God against worshippers of false gods or the ungodly wicked and the unfolding of his rewards to the righteous, or even to the humble.

The prophet Isaiah promises an oppressed but chosen people a 'New Jerusalem' of happiness and prosperity once their sins have been purged away in the collapse of the old order of corrupt and fallen Jerusalem. The satirist Aristophanes mocks democratic egalitarianism or primitive communism in the *Ecclesiazusae*, even before we can find any serious acccount of its advocacy. The rebel wife, Praxagora, tells her amazed and terrified husband:

> The rule which I dare to enact and declare
> Is that all shall be equal and equally share
> All wealth and enjoyments, nor longer endure
> That one should be rich, and another be poor . . .

If not open sex war, there was bitter class war in and among the Greek city-states and expropriation of the property of the rich after revolts by the 'demos', the many or the poor. Some cities regarded themselves as having democratic constitutions and others oligarchical or aristocratic. The Athenian leader Pericles boasted that the Athenians were unique in debating every public issue publicly and in 'ruling and being ruled in turn'.

Rulers in the Roman world both feared and courted the

power of the people. Cicero summed up the essence of the Republic's constitution as '*auctoritas in Senatus, potestas in populum*', 'authority in the Senate, power in the people'. At times there was a politics of land reform: the brothers Gracchi attempted a policy of expropriation and distribution of large estates to 'the people'. There were even slave revolts in Rome, the most famous being that of Spartacus, with his vain hope to build an ideal city commonwealth — an event which became a lasting legend, whether of hope or of fear. Yet while a fierce spirit of egalitarian democracy can be found in classical litera- ture and life, none of this was socialism. Whenever they spoke of 'populus' or 'the people', they meant those who had, on some issues, political rights and the vote, the citizens. Citizen- ship was usually coterminous with both the economic ability and the legal right to furnish and to bear arms. But in no known state in the ancient world was anything like a majority of the inhabitants, even of the adult male inhabitants, citizens. And like the prophecies of Isaiah, even the most democratic ideas of the Greeks were ideas for themselves, they could not imagine them to have universal application. Greek and Roman thinkers held that all men, women and slaves even, had some rights: but the full rights of citizenship, which represented humanity at its highest, were limited to those who had the reason and ability (which needed property and leisure) to fit them to be citizens.

The civic ideal was a great and civilizing one. The idea that a large number of people could govern themselves politically or by reasoning in public debate, not simply consulting tradition or oracles or representatives of the gods and divine order, was as big an advance in human history as working with metal, the harnessing of beasts or the invention of the compass. The Greeks were conscious of their uniqueness: that is why they called themselves the '*eleutheros*' or 'the free' and all others '*barbaroi*'. And their politics was for large numbers, at least in an important relative sense: representative institutions evolved and were invented when numbers became too large for either the direct physical coercion of tyrants and their bodyguards or for the private discussions of oligarchs and aristocrats (as it were, 'within these four palace walls' rather than oratory in the public market-place). But no one in the ancient world seriously believed that all adults could be citizens. Usually, of course, even in republics, there was a traditionally defined property franchise. And there was an almost universal justification or rationalization of it, well expressed in Aristotles' *Politics*: 'that leisure was the mother of philosophy', so that without property there was no leisure or time for real work, only the perpetual 'soul-destroying' (as we say — they would have said 'mind-destroying') labour of keeping alive; and without knowledge and reason, which were the proper fruits of leisure, there could be no skill in the art of politics and government. These ideas have had a very long run for their money. Government and politics were seen as a *'techne'*, rather as we see 'art', a mixture of hard-learned skill and knowledge and of innate qualities too. Plato held that no amount of formal training could fit some men for office, though a rigorous education was a prerequisite for the presumption to rule over others.

If 'socialism' means anything, both considering the history and usage of the concept and what a theory called 'socialist' might be invoked to claim and to explain, it is at least universalistic. 'The workers of the world' may not unite under one banner, still less form a line in front of one super-bureaucrat's desk; 'a thousand flowers may bloom' or each nation may have a 'unique path to socialism'; but within each nation or form of socialism it must at least be believed, however practice disappoints, that every adult human being is capable of making an equal contribution to the common good and should be treated equally. In the ancient world such ideas were not unknown but were fugitive and eccentric, and lacked any serious intellectual, political or social base.

The ancient world also had no clear idea of deliberate and cumulative social change for the better — the distinctively modern idea of progress. One regime was good, another bad, life was happy or unfortunate; our children's generation may be more fortunate than ours, but the next might swing back again. Cyclical theories were common: the wheel of fortune kept on turning on a fixed axis, possibly in a progression — taught Plato and then Polybius — from tyranny to democracy, but then a regression as 'demagogues' emerge from the people and become oligarchs. Apart from incidents of good or bad harvests, victory or defeat, the future will resemble the past. But the very concept of modernity is bound up with the belief, no older than the beginning of the eighteenth century in Western Europe, that the future will not resemble the past. If in Limbo or Purgatory we meet the shades of the great philosophers of antiquity, as Dante met Virgil, we will not easily understand each other.

Certainly utopias were imagined before the modern era. But like the 'New Jerusalem', they were fixed and final orders. Change, which was generally conceived, like most of the life of the body, as gradual decay, had become arrested. Sequential time was irrelevant. The modern world, as we will see, views time very differently. Also, while socialism has roots in Christianity, both in its egalitarianism and in its universalism, yet the Gospels, while preaching charity, a duty to help the poor, brotherly love and (at least according to St Luke) apostolic poverty and communism of property for the disciples and their special followers, are yet severely other-wordly: life is a pilgrimage in hope of salvation through a transitory world of pain and tears — 'My kingdom is not of this world.' Christians can be socialists but socialism is not dependent on religious belief: its predominant mode is secular — which again is unique to the modern world.

Millenial and utopian thought before the modern era only existed as forms of Christian heresy. Wars of extermination were fought both against those like the gentle Albigenses who believed that the lion was ready to lie down with the lamb and those like the militant Hussites who aimed to shatter and renew a corrupted world utterly. Norman Cohn in his *The Pursuit of the Millenium* has characterized Millenial movements and Anabaptist revolts of the later Middle Ages as 'revolutionary Messianism'. Fanatics believed in the imminence of the Apocalypse, as foretold in the book of *The Revelation* of St John the Divine, the establishment of a Final Kingdom of the Saints on Earth and the Second Coming of Jesus Christ. This Kingdom was to last for a Thousand Years and it was always 'his Saints' who were 'to inherit the earth and the fruits thereof', unhappily not you or me. Cohn describes such groups as fraternities who felt themselves to be elites. Both psychologies were equally fervid. Opinions varied as to whether Christ would rule on earth perpetually, the Gnostic heresy, or take up the Saints and the Elect to heaven, cast down all sinners and destroy the earth. The ideas of the

Elect themselves were often intensely egalitarian and fraternal, in some instances even extending to ideas of equality
between the sexes and to leadership by inspired children (the
sacredness of innocence); and they were always an open or an
implied challenge to the established hierarchies of the land-
owning aristocracy and the property-owning Church. Social
conditions of poverty, famine, disease and oppression were
among the obvious triggers for such small sectarian fantasies
to become, on occasion, momentarily plausible wild hopes;
and so for attempts to be made to realize them by fanatical
rebellion. But the motivations, concepts and visions of such
people were highly elitist and almost wholly religious (and, to
the majority of the religious, heretical). The Elect would
always be a minority and the vast majority of us, whether
rulers or workers, would be damned. This is a long way from
socialism. Such matters have perhaps excited some socialist
historians unduly.

Yet some links and essential preconditions are there. The
astounding idea of a total transformation of society was
invented by the Hebrew prophets and popularized by the early
Christians, not by Rousseau or Marx. And from the Millena-
rians came the idea that a sudden increase in widespread
suffering (what Marxists were to call 'immiseration') is a true
and clear sign that a New Era is about to break forth after a
period of violent revolutions which will burn away and uproot
the old order utterly. Also the idea of individuals undergoing a
qualitative change of state as they move into the working class
or, eventually, the classless society, would have been incomprehensible in secular terms if St Paul had not long before
characterized conversion to Christianity as a sudden and
complete being 'born again in Christ'. At times the demands
of the Communist Party in the twentieth century were to be
almost as severe as those of the Church, or rather those who
thought themselves to be the true Church militant. Some of
the children of the rich have become, in our times 'born again
socialists' (if sometimes on a sensibly part-time basis).

There is almost as much remaking as making of history.
Socialists have come to look back for the comfort of paternity
to noble ancestors in the past. But it has usually had to be a
very selective and unhistorical retrospect. Before *ideology*, no
earlier than the late eighteenth and the early nineteenth

centuries, there was *myth*. But there is no need to be a bad historian in order to be a good socialist. One can enjoy and be animated by myths and legends; yet being untrue, or at best only very partially and symbolically true, they are dangerous guides to action. Socialism could never have come into being without certain preconditions in the intellectual history of the West; but there was no socialism in the pre-modern world — the necessary conditions both for the ideology and the attempted practice are bound up with the democratic theories and events of the French Revolution and the economic events and theories of the Industrial Revolution.

The idea of democracy is both historically and logically prior to that of socialism. Socialism is a special form of democracy, it arises from a tradition of democratic ideas and, to some extent, democratic experience. Democracy is a necessary, but not a sufficient, part of any definition of socialism. But I am talking of 'democracy' in its primal, classical sense of the rule or the power of the 'demos', the poor, later of any majority, not in its nineteenth-century liberal sense. Strictly speaking the political, republican or — some would argue — the constitutional tradition is concerned with citizens not with all men and women. Very rarely did the poor have any part at all in the franchise. But at various periods the plebeians or the 'proles' of the city of Rome had exercised through a plebiscite or by elected tribunes a veto on Senatorial laws or decrees. The patrician or Senatorial class accepted this not out of any principled belief in popular rights, but out of a realistic recognition of popular power: if harnessed, it gave the Roman State unique strength, while attempts to suppress it were perpetually destablizing (as Machiavelli was to argue). All this was remembered by scholars and statesmen as part of the political tradition of the West, even remembered in feudal parliaments and in the courts of absolute kings. In the pre-modern world, what history there was seemed very close and at times frighteningly reversible. This primal sense of democracy also had little to do with individualism or any belief that each biological individual has identical rights, still less that these rights include political rights or 'liberty'.

Today we tend to confuse the concepts of majority rule, individual rights and liberty. We lump them together with conceptual optimism in 'democracy' as a catch-all concept or as a fig-leaf for State power. But each can exist on its own and can be hostile to the others. Lenin's 'dictatorship of the proletariat' and the Jacobin 'sovereignty of the people', for instance, both claimed to be democratic in a majoritarian sense and to override, until the end of an endless emergency, all individual rights and liberties. Few of the famous *philosophes* of the French enlightenment were democrats at all, but they all believed in the utmost liberty for the educated against both church and state, and in lesser rights for others. Like the English Whigs, they believed in universal equality before the law but that the law should restrict the political franchise in the interests of property and social hierarchy. There were even some who thought that individual rights (whether of conscience or property) could best be protected by an enlightened ruler or ruling class, but with no general liberty to criticize or to rubbish a benign and benevolent state. More commonly it came to be believed that a written and entrenched constitution, binding the rulers themselves, could protect liberty against democracy and egalitarianism (as in the nineteenth-century middle class German ideal of a *Rechtsstaat* and the Federalist reading of the United States constitution).

Certainly some socialists have in practice used the concept of class to give an even greater override to the majority, now sanctified as *the* working class — and their leaders. But neither the doctrine nor the theory could be held to be universally true unless everyone was regarded as inherently equal, however much institutional power has corrupted some men with illusions of qualitative difference. Both modern democracy and socialism needed an argument to show why *everyone* should have political rights and could be a citizen, not just those who were chosen, especially fit, knowledgeable or educated. Radical liberals in the nineteenth-century said 'give every man (perhaps women) a minimum of property, or help them to it', and a fully democratic franchise could work safely. The 'philosophic liberals', like John Stuart Mill, said that if universal and compulsory secondary education were instituted, then and only then democracy would work. With education even the indigenous inhabitants of India would, one day many generations hence, be fit for representative self-government. But this whole Aristotelean, classical, Whiggish premise, that objective attainments were needed for citizenship, had already been challenged. The challenge was not in itself socialist, but was an essential precondition to socialism and underlies it to this day.

From where did Robert Burns get the extraordinary idea when he declaimed those words that should never be allowed to become banal or lose their force?

> For a'that, and a'that,
> It's comin' yet, for a'that,
> That man to man, the world o'er
> Shall brothers be for a'that. . . .

From French republicans and Scottish sympathizers, of course; but they in turn from Rousseau. Before Rousseau and for some time after 'a'that' had always meant at least a minimal property franchise and an assumption of some objective knowledge. Noble forbears who sound like modern democrats to us, even like putative socialists, when they attack with great vigour and knowing an existing property franchise, more often turn out to be advocating simply a lower property franchise.

In the famous debate at Putney in 1647–49 of the Parliamentary Army Council between the Generals Cromwell and Ireton and the elected 'Agitators' of the regiments, we can hear:

> The poorest he that is in England has a life to live as the greatest. . . . There are many thousands of us soldiers that have ventured our lives; we have but little property in the kingdom, yet we have a birthright. And it now seems that you argue that unless a man has a fixed estate in the kingdom, he has no right in the kingdom. I wonder we were so much deceived. . . .
>
> *Ireton*. Truly no man can take from you your birthright, but in civil society there are laws and a constitution as well as birthright, and no man has a birthright to the property of another. If all men vote equally, many shall soon pass to taking hold of the property of other men.
>
> *Rainborough*. Sir, I see that it is impossible to have liberty but all property must be taken away. If it be laid down for a rule, and if you say it, it must be so.

But Rainborough is not advocating the confiscation of property; he is angrily mocking one *reductio ad absurdum* with another. And even the famous Levellers who did argue that 'all men vote equally', and were thus beloved in popular books on the rise of both democracy and of socialism, specifically excluded, modern scholars now sadly reveal, all servants, debtors and tenants of rented property. None of these could be truly 'independent' because each would be under the economic power of another. To be truly a man you need 'a' that' as well. 'Independency' was thus not the same as egalitarianism and to be striven for by a mass movement, as libertarian socialists would later argue, but was itself the precondition of such movements.

How could it be that, to return to Burns, 'a man's a man for a' that', that a person can even be a citizen without possessing any preconditions of knowledge, property or education? The bohemian Rousseau gave an astonishing answer: if you and I have sincerity, moral courage and simplicity, and can thus cast out both self-interest and artificial conventions. Thus purified and equipped each of us can will (not reason or calculate) what is good for us in general. What is good for all is what we can each find in our heart and sensibility when we act unselfishly and naturally. The Will, not Reason, still less a new artificial Education or old Faith, is what makes us each human and ensures a common humanity. Put simply, the heart and not the head should rule. Each us should and can cultivate simplicity not sophistication.

The doctrine of the general will has been subject to endless mockery from the time of his sceptical contemporary, Voltaire, to endless student essays hunting for what is easily found, even in Rousseau's finest works — contradiction and extravagant assertions. But it is hard to live without him. He cuts Aristotle's Gordian knot tying reason and citizenship with leisure and property. Why should all men and women have an equal vote (when abilities and understanding vary so greatly) and why should we think at all that all people are of equal worth? The Christian says because we are all children of one father, but Rousseau says because we are all by nature capable of fraternity or fellow-feeling. We develop this by meeting people, talking to them, living with them in communities. This is, of course, a secularized and socialized (romanticized some would say) version of the Christian doctrines of 'soul' and of 'conscience'. Without Christianity there would be no Rousseau or romantic sensibility and without Rousseau no socialism. But each is very different from the other, even if never wholly exclusive.

The philosopher Kant once said that 'two things never cease to move me with wonder, the starry heavens above and the moral law within'. Newton was the philosopher of the first and Rousseau of the second.

In his great essay *On Eternal Peace* of 1795 Kant paid a more specific tribute to Rousseau.

> I am myself by inclination a seeker after truth . . . There was a time when I thought that this alone could constitute the highest object of mankind and I despised the common man who knows nothing. Rousseau set me right. This blind prejudice vanished; I learned to respect human nature and I should consider myself far more worthless than the average workingman if I did not believe that this idea underlies all others in establishing the rights of man.

Thus Rousseau was seen as prophet of the rights of man and the idealizer of the common man. The 'common man' was not quite 'the workingman', he was more of a superior peasant, small shopkeeper or craftsman; and he was versatile, he could turn his own hands to anything. Rousseau railed against the rich, or the excessively rich, but the answer to acute poverty was honest toil and the cultivation of simplicity and republican virtues. Neither class nor property were in themselves denounced, only their abuse in pride, luxury and power. 'Wealth should never be so great that a man can buy his neighbour, nor so lacking that a man is compelled to sell himself . . .' A solid and enduring state 'must have neither millionaires nor beggars . . .' Nonetheless the moral attributes of his somewhat rural, certainly pre-industrial, common man could easily be transferred to the class-conscious urban workingman.

In another respect too he laid some of the foundations of socialism. In his didactic novel *Emile* of 1762, written in the same year as *The Social Contract*, a prophetic voice sometimes takes over:

> You who trust in the present order of society can scarcely conceive that this order is subject to inevitable revolutions whose effects upon your children are impossible to foretell! The great ones become small, the rich turn poor, the monarch becomes a subject: are the blows of fate so rare that you may count on being exempt from them? We approach the state of crisis and the century of Revolutions!

This could still be no more modern and just as medieval as the language of the *Magnificat* where the casting down of the great and the exalting of the oppressed is a traditional threat to the bad great and hope for the good poor — something quite remote, however, from any modern aggregation of individual souls into social class. But his talk of revolutions seems something more than another turn of the classical fixed wheel of fortune. His wheel must be moving up and on, not just spinning on its axis, for he is saying that the common man is actually morally superior to the lord, the bishop and even to the scholar. The future could be very different, at first terrible in its convulsions but then splendid in its outcome. And events can be shaped, we do not simply have to endure and hope for a heavenly reward. The idea of progress is dawning and future revolutions may lead to permanent betterment for all, to a new order of human society not just to the violent and recurrent reversal of the established fortunes of some.

In two other respects Rousseau revealed ambivalences or contradictions that were both to animate and haunt future socialists. For man to be free he must be an active citizen bound not by imposed laws or 'chains' but by his own virtue, his own voluntary willing of the general will. Morality is not a command from God or a social superior on earth, it is a voluntary recognition of fellowship. But what if a man cannot succeed in willing generally, willing for the common good, what if he cannot rid himself of economic self-interest or partiality to friends or family? Then, said Rousseau famously,

> Whosoever shall refuse to obey the general will must be constrained by the whole body of his fellow citizens to do so: which is no more than to say that it may be necessary to force a man to be free — freedom being that condition which, by giving each citizen to his country, guarantees him from all personal dependence and is the foundation upon which the whole political machine rests, and supplies the power which works it.

But whatever freedom is, it is not that. Freedom may conflict with quite justifiable social obligations. Better to say that I am not free to exploit my workers than to say that I am more free when I am forced to treat them properly. We have to balance the common good against individual freedom. Morality and freedom are not the same thing. It was a dangerous if innocent and incidental argument on Rousseau's part. But that kind of logic was to lead many an old Bolshevik to feel that it was impossible to be right against the Party or to be free to question its wisdom. It was to recreate in a secular form the dilemma of the sceptic or the unorthodox in the Church from which Rousseau was trying to escape. More generally it fed the idea that freedom and virtue are quite indistinguishable if the cause is good.

Rousseau was profoundly ambivalent about the size of community in which the general will could flourish. He favoured direct democracy and deeply distrusted representation. He had an idealized vision of the Greek city-states as being small 'face to face' societies of public-spirited citizens who, knowing each other's characters well, had little need for formal law. 'The immense size of states, foreign conquests, and the abuse by Government of its functions, all these things have encouraged that innovation by which deputies or representatives are held to act for the People in the assemblies of the nation.' Power, he believes, cannot be delegated, and the consequences of trying are dire: 'As soon as a man thinking of the affairs of state says: "They don't concern me", it is time to conclude that the State is lost.' He did, with rare practicality, admit that small States can fall prey to their neighbours, and in a footnote he promised in a future work to show 'how the external strength of a great People may be combined with the convenient polity and the solid order of a small State' by considering 'the nature of confederations — a new subject, and one of which the principles have yet to be established'. Indeed.

The dilemma is not unique to socialists that small-scale government, while constituting a participative education in civic spirit, is weak to powerful neighbours who fear that good example may spread, and even on a large scale representative government tends to centralization and bureaucracy. The American founding fathers in 1787 debated the question anxiously and reached a sensible and long-lasting federal compromise. But the question has a special poignancy for socialists, unanticipated by Rousseau, when a strong, centralized State is needed for economic development as well as defence, and yet the cooperative small group, commune, worker's council or Soviet best exemplifies the practical ethics of socialism. Not merely were there to be the extremes of anarchism and of Lenin's despotism, but even within democratic Socialism the debate between centralizers and decentralizers has raged fiercely in many different forms and with varying fortunes.

The two themes of freedom and the general will and of size and scale also reflect the dilemma, especially intense for Rousseau, but present in all subsequent ultra-democratic and socialist thinkers, of balancing the claims of individuality and sociability. I become myself at my best by being liberated from an artificial society and from extremes of poverty or wealth, but above all by sociability, by honest, sincere, benevolent and fraternal interaction with similar human beings; and they constitute a collective conscience. But I am also, as he challenges us in his *Confessions*, absolutely unique:

> Myself alone! I know the feelings of my heart, and I know men. I am not made like any of those I have seen; I venture to believe that I am not made like any of those in existence. If I am not better, at least I am different.

Each man and woman must then, according to Rousseau, develop not conventional good character, learning or status, but personality. But will 'community' enhance this or prove a new form of oppression? Small groups of *authentic* (has became the fashionable word) and sincere personalities trying to live together fraternally are to some a vision of true humanity, but to others of an intrusive hell. There was to develop, on the one hand, a 'collective-consciousness' school of socialism (the party or the movement as a whole knows best), and, on the other, an anarchist school (you all exist for me, or at least we all exist to admire each other). Strangely both these contrary views have their roots, or at least their first and most eloquent dual expression, in the writings of Jean Jacques Rousseau. His bust was to be placed on the table of the Jacobin Club in the brief but never to be forgotten days of their rule.

2

The Great Revolution

Leszek Kolakowski in his magisterial history, *Main Currents of Marxism*, asks what were the common elements of socialist thought when Karl Marx first began to write in the 1840s. They were, he says:

> . . . the conviction that the uncontrolled concentration of wealth and unbridled competition was bound to lead to increasing misery and crises, and that the system must be replaced by one in which the organisation of production and exchange could do away with poverty and oppression and bring about a redistribution of the world's gifts on a basis of equality.

But replaced how? And how did such an astounding hope ever arise? By the time that socialist theory emerged from among inchoate, disparate and often bizarre egalitarian doctrines, the presumption was already overwhelming that it would be through revolution. Men more often think from analogy than from abstract reason, especially when the analogous situations are close at hand. The events and then the memory and legend of the French Revolution, or '*La Grande Revolution*' as it was more often called in Europe until 1917, made that phrase ambiguous, dominated European politics for ever after and spread around the world. Few people saw it as finished business (like Nazism with the defeat and death of Hitler): it might recur as an event and its effects had not ended as an historical process.

The objects of the revolution were at first constitutional, to reform France to be like England, no worse, possibly a little better: to limit the powers of the monarch and to abolish the censorship by the permanent institution of a National Assembly of the traditional three estates of the realm: the nobility, the clergy and the bourgeoise or the third estate, only the latter to be reconstituted on a rational property franchise intended to favour the educated, at the very most the actively literate. But as reforms were granted too late and as expectations were aroused, outbursts of popular grievances passed beyond the control of constitutional moderates; and a vague but passionate opinion began to form in favour of uprooting and replacing the old order itself. The uprooting was clearer in men's minds than the replacement: the old nobility was to be abolished, the power of the Church destroyed, and the lands of both confiscated and distributed; the monarchy was to be put under popular control, and, when it resisted, destroyed; but somehow the censorship, which was to have been destroyed in the name of liberty, became retained in the name of fraternity, but purified and put into the hands of patriotic leaders of enlightened virtue. The attack was launched with a deep-felt rhetoric of 'liberty and equality', to which 'fraternity' became added as the moral virtue (and, in times of crisis, a psychological reality) which must link the two. The 'rights of man' and 'the sovereignty of the people' became powerful, associated additions.

Even the first great historian of the Revolution, Alexis de Tocqueville, spoke of a conscious intention to substitute for the residues of feudalism 'a more uniform and simpler state of society and politics, based upon equality of social condition'. This 'equality' was not, however, economic equality but simply, though astounding and emancipatory enough, equality before the law. And still 'the people' seen as citizens were by no means a majority: women were not enfranchised and nor were the very poor, the *sans culottes*, nor hired rural labourers, nor publicly designated 'enemies of the people'. The lack of political equality in the revolution and the reality of continued economic deprivation were obscured, in times of crisis at least (and crises were rarely lacking and, if so, easy to produce), by the doctrine of fraternity and the sudden burgeoning of a public ethic of simplicity of manners and conduct set by the example of noble and patriotic public figures. The common people were stirred up first against the old regime, then by popular leaders against each other and finally against all foreign enemies of the people, the Revolution and France. The power of the people, particularly of the city mob, was demonstrated and was managed but was not made part of a permanent, peace-time constitution. Some leaders could be specially honoured for having come from the poor but a permanent voice for the poor would threaten property rights. Bread could be distributed in time of famine at public expense but otherwise the price of bread must obey the rational, happily impersonal and newly discovered natural laws of economics. '*Citoyen*' became the universal form of address, and fraternity felt real so long as the young republic was under threat.

Napoleon created a new aristocracy, but of talent, not of birth. Equality of opportunity became the watchword even as he suppressed political democracy and silenced the old Jacobins: the way to the top was to be opened to all by universal education, and a Marshal's baton was in the knapsack of every common soldier. Because Napoleon inherited the patriotic, nationalistic fervour of the revolution, he could trust the common people with arms. That was the political basis of his military power. His *levée en masse* was a democratic device: none of the autocracies he fought, nor Britain neither, dared trust their common people with arms: their systems of conscription, if they existed at all, had to be highly selective. 'The politics of the future', said Napoleon, 'will be the art of stirring the masses.' Politics in the past had been the art of encouraging sleeping dogs to lie still. Modern war as well as modern industry needed a more democratic, nationalistic and mobilised political order.

The Revolution was the greatest emancipatory event in European history (or rather, series of events). It profoundly effected the future of the socialist movement but it was not in itself socialist. Both the Girondists and the Jacobins believed in freeing the market from the restraints of the old order: economic liberalism and an enforcement of individual property rights were the order of the day. Danton's economics were limited to favouring division of the lands of the Church and the old aristocracy, but otherwise natural ability must be rewarded. Nonetheless, the movement was both profoundy democratic compared to anything attempted on this scale ever before and by token of the fear it created in governments elsewhere in Europe, or hope among the enlightened. 'Bliss was it in this dawn to be alive', sang Wordsworth, briefly and rashly, 'And to be young, was very heaven.' For unlike the American Revolution, it promised or threatened to create an international movement.

'The American Revolution' was more truly a 'War of Independence': existing self-governing colonies asserted traditional
rights against new attempts at effective imperial control. There
was no existing feudal order to destroy in North America and
no new class came to power during or after the revolution. The
circumstances and culture of the British North American
colonies were so peculiar that not until the mid-nineteenth
century did reformers elsewhere begin to think of the American
system as something to be copied or adapted, rather than
America as a place of tolerant refuge for political exiles or men
and women seeking 'to better themselves'. Even American
historians who were once eager to say that if theirs had not been
a real revolution, 'what had?', soon became, for the most part,
also eager to say that the revolution *had* taken place, concluded
its historic business, and would not be needed again. Jefferson,
it was soon felt, had been too Francophile or simply melodramatic, almost un-American, to say that 'in every generation
the tree of liberty needs manuring with the blood of patriots'.
The tradition of the French Revolution, however, was that it
would (or could) recur everywhere, and even in France to this
day many people speak as if its business is unfinished. The
Great Revolution had not failed, it had been betrayed! Where
revolutions elsewhere only have limited success, it is only
because the old leaders become corrupted by power when there
are no new patriots to chasten or pull them down!

Tocqueville was to characterize the internationalism of the
revolution in a memorable passage of his *L'ancien regime en
France*:

> The French Revolution was then a political revolution, which in its
> operation and aspect resembled a religious one. It had every peculiar
> and characteristic feature of a religious movement: it not only spread
> to foreign countries, but it was carried thither by preaching and by
> propaganda. It is impossible to conceive of a stranger spectacle than
> that of a political revolution which inspired proselytism, which its
> adherents preach to foreigners with as much ardour and passion as
> they have shown in enacting it at home . . . As it affected to tend more
> towards the regeneration of mankind than ever towards the reform of
> France, it roused passions such as the most violent political revolu-
> tions had never before excited.

From Rousseau had come the idea of the universality of the
rights of man: the great shift in human belief from the wisdom

of rulers to the will of the common people. Almost in one leap France passed from a system of authority based on passive obedience and dynastic loyalty into an active popular enthusiasm for national identity which, in turn, for a dramatic decade, seemed about to become an international principle.

The idea of nationalism was new enough — that for every nation there must be a state and that rulers must not merely be popular but of their people; and it first saw the light of day in the claim that all Europe should throw off dynastic allegiances and create national republics. Alas, it was the nationalist element of this unprecedented amalgam that proved the most potent. Dynasts hurried to redress and represent themselves as national monarchs, defenders of the traditional cultures of their loving peoples against — it became — the cosmopolitan deism or atheism of the French. But many of the best minds among their councillors, while fighting the French, learned much from them: unhappily more from Napoleon's endeavour to create a rational system of central administration than from the confused, violent but heroic attempts to create popular representative institutions. Tolstoy in *War and Peace* was to picture André and Pierre as each agonizingly torn between traditional love of country and intellectual admiration for Napoleon and the 'French principles' of humanity's future.

Is there really some remorseless logic in all revolutions which follows what was later asserted to be the pattern of the Great Revolution: the time of spontaneous protest, popular liberties and moderate constitutional reform; then the resistance of the old regime and the coming to power of extremists — the representatives of popular power becoming the controllers of popular power; then the sacrifice of liberty and the imposition of terror to purify and accelerate the revolution; then the beginning of bloodshed among the revolutionary leaders themselves ('the revolution devours its children' — as in Büchner's drama, *Danton's Death*); and finally the counter-revolution, either from outside, or an internal reaction, diluting the original ideology and restoring stability, all in the name of the revolution but led by a new despot imposing a post-revolutionary status quo? Or does this, itself partly mythic pattern, create the very language in which we talk about, the very concepts by which we perceive, all future revolutions? It is hard to escape from the spell of the Great

Revolution. Before that nobody had believed that the values of a society could be changed by popular rebellion towards those of a rational, secular, free and (in some sense) egalitarian order.

Conservatives like Edmund Burke in England and De Maistre in France could never quite decide whether the idea of revolution was impossible, and that the bloodshed and terror stemmed from trying to do the impossible; or whether it was all too possible to create such an undesirable, rational, egalitarian, totally new and — both men agreed — godless regime. But they drew comfort from the immediate failure of the revolution in France, even if, from that time onwards, probably the deepest fear of conservatives has been not an alternative iron order (or even a just and benign one), but the breakdown of any order at all as a necessary consequence of all such large-scale attempts at betterment. To the true conservative, any kind of order is preferable to the risk of anarchy; while to the true revolutionary, obsessed with the injustice and suffering of an old order, almost anything is worth trying. One does not need to be clear where one is going: if the old, artificial, oppressive and corrupting order is smashed, beyond it lies a natural order peopled by natural men. The ghost of Rousseau will wash the blood from the hands of Robespierre.

Marx was to be appalled by such 'utopian', he usually said, fantasies and visions about the means towards admittedly utopian ends. That is why he wished for a 'scientific socialism'. But such beliefs are very hard to eradicate. William Blake was not alone in sniffing the balm of a New Jerusalem in at least the first smoke of the French Revolution.

> I will not cease from Mental Fight,
> Nor shall my Sword sleep in my hand
> Till we have built Jerusalem
> In England's green & pleasant Land.

Read properly, it is the greatest revolutionary hymn in the English language. Or as he ended his prophetic 'Song of Liberty' in 1793 itself: 'EMPIRE IS NO MORE! AND NOW THE LION & WOLF SHALL CEASE.' But, alas, the lion and lamb have stubbornly refused even to lie down together.

All revolutions have shown the tensions that existed in Rousseau's pre-revolutionary thought: a spontaneous individualism that feels smothered by established conventions wrestling desperately with the desire to impose a new sociability that none may evade. 'Those who are not for us are against us', cried St Just as the Assembly tried to debate the decisions of the Committee of Public Safety, 'what are they but enemies of the people?' The fearsome phrase was born. And 'what do people want who want neither virtue nor terror?' Almost as soon as *les philosophes*, the old literary and learned critics of the old regime, had popularized ideas of freedom of speech and tolerance, even of judicial neutrality and impartiality, these ideas were challenged in the name of the safety and welfare of 'the sovereign people' — challenged by their leaders. Robespierre explained:

> The terror is nothing but justice, prompt, severe and inflexible, it is thus an emanation of virtue; it is less a special principle than a consequence of the general principle of democracy applied to the most pressing needs of our country.

But there is no reason why all revolutions should yield the same result, unless we do believe in inevitable patterns. (Orwell once remarked that all revolutions are failures, but that they are not all the same kind of failures.)

Nonetheless there is an everlasting poignancy in the picture that the great Liberal Lord Acton painted in his *Lectures on the French Revolution* of what befell the philosophic author of the first coherent account of the concept 'progress' — that not merely will the future be better than the past but that there are laws of history and society which point towards a growing and cumulative betterment.

> During the agony of his party [the purge of the Gironde by the Jacobins] Condorcet found shelter in a lodging house in Paris. There, under the reign of terror, he wrote a little book on human progress . . . There may be, perhaps, a score or two dozen decisive and characteristic views that govern the world, and that every man should master in order to understand his age, and this is one of them. When the book was finished, the author's part was played and he had nothing more to live for. As his retreat was known to one, at least, of the Montagnards, he feared to compromise those who had taken him in at the risk of their lives. Condorcet assumed a disguise, and crept out of the house with a Horace in one pocket and a dose of poison in the other . . . A few miles outside Paris he was arrested on suspicion and lodged in the gaol. In the morning they found him lying dead.

Acton thought that all revolutions necessarily do more harm than good. He sweepingly claimed, exaggerating greatly, that the Jacobins habitually came to substitute 'happiness' for 'liberty' in their rhetoric, retaining only 'equality' and 'fraternity' (which for Acton seemed to mean perpetual association with the wrong sort of people). In fact most of them held the normal view that they would have read about in the annals of republican Rome, to which all reformers (both revolutionaries and moderates) turned as the only possible precedent: that liberty could be suspended for the time of the emergency, that dictatorship was a temporary, republican and constitutional office. Indeed the old books said that a dictator who artificially prolongs the emergency to perpetuate his power becomes, *ipso facto*, an outlaw and it is the duty of patriots to arrest or kill him. Easier said than done. But they never doubted that the purpose of the revolution was to extend and enhance popular liberties; and that 'revolutionary legality' was an event in time, not a continuous and self-perpetuating process.

The tumult of any revolution produces some extreme ideas on its fringes which may, if the memory of them survives, prove — in hindsight — important. One proto-socialist at least emerged in the conspiracy of Gracchus Babeuf in 1796 against the reaction of the Directory after the fall of Robespierre and the Jacobins. His fellow conspirator Buonarroti survived to write in his famous *Conspiration pour l'egalite dite Babeuf* (1828) that Babeuf believed that 'the perpetual cause of the enslavement of peoples is nothing but inequality, and as long as it exists the assertion of national rights will be illusory as far as the masses of people are concerned, sunk as they are beneath the level of human dignity'. Before there could be liberty and rights for all, property had to be taken from the rich and divided equally among the poor. This, he naively assumed, would remedy the main cause of poverty. The doctrine is clear, a primitive communism, even if the theory is thin. These ideas had no effect and little following at the time. But once one traditional order had been destroyed, however confusing and paradoxical were the immediate results, 'the lid could never be put back on Pandora's box', as conservatives were wont to say.

Ideas only become powerful when conditions are right. But

conditions do not create ideas. That is why this account is
mainly about ideas. The growth of cities, of a capitalist market
and of industrialism (themselves related but by no means identical phenomena) create the conditions for egalitarian and
libertarian ideas to flourish in the form of socialist doctrines,
even theories. 'The Revolution' was the trigger to all these
subsequent ideas and movements. Consider the famous
anecdote that Louis XVI on hearing of the storming of the
Bastille on 14 July 1789, said to the Duke of Rochefoucauld-
Liancourt, '*C'est une revolte?*' and received (according to the
Duke's own memoirs) the prescient reply, '*Non, Sire, c'est une
revolution.*' It is reasonably clear what the Duke meant in
hindsight; but what could he have meant at the time? We
should pause, even anticipate, to ask what was and is meant by
'revolution'.

A revolution was, to make sense of the Duke's remark,
clearly something more than '*une revolte*', even '*une grande
revolte*'. *Une revolte* could damage the interests, properties
and lives of particular nobles or officials and their families,
and *une grande revolte* could be aimed at changing the policies
of or capturing the Crown itself; but it was still not an attempt
to change the customary values and practices of a whole
society. To call any illegal, sudden and violent change of
government a 'revolution' is comprehensible; but it fails to
make an important distinction between those revolts concerned
with political and those concerned with social change. 'Revolution', in its modern sense, that is since the French Revolution, distinctively carries the connotation of social change.
However, King Louis could only have thought that the Duke
meant, at the time, that he and his family were going to be
overthrown, a violent reversal of fortune.

For originally revolution meant no more than the Roman
'*revolare*', any sudden turning of fortune for a state, city,
government, or even great individual. The Romans used the
concept much as modern translators strive to catch the meaning of the Greek '*stasis*': seizures of power that were sudden,
unstable, self-perpetuatingly unstable, the very antithesis of
good government of any kind — that chronic, endemic insta-
bility that was described in the pages of Thucydides or is found
today in the dreary cycle in parts of Africa and South America
when one damned military *coup d'état* succeeds another.

The idea arose in classical and renaissance times that there were some cyclical, inevitable patterns in government: a general tendency for the form of government, in the absence of good rule, to swing from autocracy to democracy and back again. Demagogues stirred the people against tyrants, then themselves became tyrants, provoking other demagogues who ... (All wise men, of course, sought for Aristotle's *via media*, the middle way which would prove stable by taking the best from aristocracy and the best from democracy.) The great wheel of fortune just kept on turning or, as a modern blues' singer would put it, 'Sometimes I'm up, sometimes I'm down, But always I'm just a-wandering round the town.' Life was like that, full of incident and changes of fortune, but basically repetitive and getting nowhere in particular. And those ancient revolutions only directly affected the ruling classes. Society was remarkably little affected by such affairs of state. There was no idea or intention of premeditated social change.

> Kings may come and kings may go
> But we go on for ever,

said the peasantry. Thus there was no sense of progress in the pre-modern concept of revolution, indeed the contrary: the belief was widespread that cycles of forms of government, famine and abundance, and fortune and misfortune were inevitable.

Not until the French and the Scottish enlightenment, thus even before the Revolution, did the concept of progress emerge. The idea began to grow that if the standards of reason, science, tolerance and freedom of expression advanced by writers like Voltaire and Diderot and found in the great *L'Encyclopédie* became generally accepted, not merely would there be a better society, in the negative sense of removing superstition, bigotry censorship, privilege and arbitrary government, but that positive conditions would then be created for continuous future betterment. The obvious vehicle was literacy and universal education. Voltaire, who was himself no democrat, distrusted the ignorance of the common man and thought that the great chariot of progress needed a driver prepared to use the whip on occasion, an 'enlightened ruler' or even a 'benevolent despot'. He briefly cast Catherine of Russia in this too demanding role. In Beethoven's *Fidelio* the messenger announces, 'The King says, "let all men be my brothers!" ' Very good of him. Condorcet, a thinker so advanced that he even thought that women had equal rights, believed, as most nineteenth-century liberals were to do, that full democracy could only follow, never precede, compulsory secondary education. Rousseau's genius lay in his challenging the very foundations of the ideology of the educated. Only by each acting like brothers (and sisters) can the brotherhood of man be created: it is not a gift, especially from kings and rulers. His humble disciples were fond of remarking that only the person who wears the shoe knows where it pinches.

The French Revolution made the belief in progress, indeed in universal reason and the rights of man, a matter of public policy, and if not in a fully democratic manner, at least in a manner radically more democratic than suited either the old autocrats or Voltaire. The men and women of the revolution did not lose sight of liberty either in their doctrines or their rhetoric, either among themselves or as an example to others in the future — even if the Jacobins compromised it fatally in the first attempt at practice. Conservative writers in Germany and Tories in England saw 'progress' as simply a sophisticated excuse for the terror, which they blamed quite simply on unrestrained, untrammeled or unfettered liberty. Later sympathizers with the Revolution, like Büchner in his great play *Danton's Death*, tended to say that it was not liberty that had got out of hand but violence. Control of the violence of the State had fallen into too few hands and it was used excessively and as a substitute for politics, not just as its last defence. Violence was needed to overthrow oppressors but was both wrong and useless as a way of spreading and consolidating new ideas and codes of conduct.

Yet the idea of progress was not discredited by the failure of the Revolution. From then on it spread rapidly and became, until the shadows of world war, mass unemployment and the nuclear bomb fell upon us, almost universally believed: simply that the future would be different from and better than the past. The Revolution was thus bound up with a fundamental condition of modernity: the possibility of conscious change for the better. And it was believed to be, if not strictly inevitable, somehow immanent or latent in human nature and society. Three things held it back, oppression, greed and ignorance. If they could be removed, whether by revolutionary violence or by education and persuasion, mankind would move towards a golden age.

Karl Marx was the first to add to the idea of revolution for freedom and progress an argument that such progress was both inevitable and economically expansive. Not just knowledge would expand but the economy too, not as a direct product of applied knowledge and invention but because of a changing pattern of class ownership of the means of production. Future societies would be wealthier in aggregate and each individual both wealthier and equally wealthy.

An anarchist tradition of socialism, however, was to go back to Rousseau and make popular spontaneity the mark of a true revolution. Only by emancipating themselves could the masses avoid a new despotism. Leadership, however dedicated to the cause, was inimicable to both liberty and equality. Anarchists saw the Jacobin 'fraternity' of common citizenship as a manipulated fraud, a shallow rhetoric of speech and dress that hid the real power relationships. Some socialists came to think that 'the revolution' need not be an event at a point in time but could be a process through time, a product of people uncompetitively cooperating together in small productive and distributive groups. Another school of anarchists differed fundamentally as to the way forward, having come to believe that there was a good and, as it were, purgative and emancipatory violence: the old order was so artificial that its apparent iron strength was, in fact, brittle, so that a sudden blow struck at the right place and at the right moment could shatter it utterly. When the old edifice collapsed the need for enforceable laws would vanish and unrepressed human nature spontaneously flourish.

Perhaps Marx takes over some part of anarchist thought in that to him the proletarian revolution would be the last revolution, and would be qualitatively different from the feudal or the bourgeois capitalist revolutions. The French revolution fell in the last category. The last revolution would be sudden and violent (with a few possible exceptions) and utterly transforming. It would transform the social structure. The rule of a self-conscious working class will briefly precede the emergence of a truly classless society, but in that final form of society (as with the anarchists) freedom and spontaneity will replace imposed laws. In Marx's day the argument between himself and the other schools of socialism was usually put in terms of the problem of the transition, not of ends.

In fact no society has ever been totally transformed. To understand any post-revolutionary society we need to understand what happened before as well as what actually happened, and what is claimed to have happened, afterwards. Nothing happens quite as is hoped for beforehand or later claimed. Tocqueville, in studying the French Revolution, first taught us to look for the causes of revolutions in the decay of authority and the incompetence of an old order, rather than in the principles advanced by the contemporary critics and then by future leaders. Here I must invoke Crick's celebrated 'iron law of revolutions': 'that revolutions take place because governments break down'; or more elaborately: 'revolutions (in so far as they are revolutions) take place not for the reasons that the party that happens to come to power during the chaos of a revolutionary situation subsequently employs corrupt historians to give out, but because the previous system of authority (how the few can govern the many) failed and collapsed.'

It will be rightly objected that my iron law is either a truism or a tautology. But at least it guides one away from abstract and rationalistic questions of how far a post-revolutionary government has fulfilled the expectations of pre-revolutionary thinkers and leads one back to important historical questions of why the old regime broke down. Failed conservatives too often blame revolutionaries for their own ineptness. Violence (as Hannah Arendty has argued) is a sign of the breakdown of political power, not its normal mode of operation. Someone has to, and will, pick up the pieces if established governments, who have every advantage and opportunity, so misgovern that they lose popular authority and, indeed, provoke, sometimes almost force, their own people into rebellion. Socialist doctrine can often mislead about the causes of revolutions, but socialist theories have a lot to say about the conditions of misgovernment.

Any revolution, including the Great Revolution, needs viewing in two ways: as an event or a series of events in a fairly precise time; and as a process that may continue through all subsequent time. The French Revolution failed to create a new, just and lasting social order. But it opened up new hopes and ideas everywhere. The idea even emerged that there could be a conscious but gradual move towards much the same goals of 'Liberty, Equality and Fraternity': the apparent paradox of an evolutionary or gradualist revolution.

3

Early Socialism

If we must think of history as having stages, whether these stages are held to be in the nature of things or our own mental constructs, yet one stage can never completely replace that which went before: something of the old order or of the old beliefs always intermingles with the new. Social history is often a better guide than the futuristic rhetoric of socialist doctrine. Hegel spoke about stages *subsuming* their predecessors, not totally replacing or cancelling them out.

'Early socialism' is not simply the first cluster of socialist doctrines, it is a set of values and beliefs that has never wholly vanished (indeed is undergoing something of a revival), even if always in different dress. 'Primitive' or 'community' socialism might better convey what is meant, if by primitive one understands 'basic'. Perhaps to call it 'pre-Marxian' is clearest, but even then to mean something that continued to underlie even the most dogmatic Marxian socialism, so that it could become post-Marxian or neo-Marxian wherever and whenever Marxism finally loses its excessive rigidity and pseudo-scientific aspirations to totality. A modern 'early socialism' is, of course, more likely to take the form of municipal socialism, inner-city cooperatives, decentralized workers' control or of Ivan Illich's de-schooled, computer-lined voluntary learning centres rather than of Fourier's agrarian *Phalansteres*; and some radical ecologists and 'Greens' claim to be socialists — and some not.

In 1841 a British working class immigrant in Ohio prophetically called William Morris wrote home to his brother in Wigan: 'I have been informed that you have gained some steps of reform in England and that there is a new society there called Sochilestes which have increased very fast and got very numerous. Please let us know if there is many of them about . . .' Notice that he said 'society' and not 'party' and that to judge by the spelling, which otherwise was sound, he had more likely heard the name than read it.

Who and what were these 'sochilestes'? They would probably have been some kind of followers of the philanthropic manufacturer Robert Owen (1771–1859). The Owenites were not revolutionaries but people who believed that production and general prosperity could be best enhanced by the collective regulation of factories and workshops on a cooperative basis. Or possibly the Ohio settler had encountered the ideas of Charles Fourier (1772–1837) or his disciples. Fourier had advocated, with crazy over-precision and fantastical detail, rural cooperatives to spread and overgrow all society, eventually even the cities. Owen wanted a cooperative mode of factory system, but Fourier hated industrialism and hoped that it would fade away. Yet both thought that 'the system', now seen as 'the capitalist system' rather than 'the old regime', could be changed from within, without seizing the state or shattering violently the old social order. Indeed neither saw control of the state as the key question: its largely malign influence could be by-passed and eroded by the creation of new types of social community.

The concept was very new. G.D.H. Cole in the first volume of his *History of Socialist Thought* says that the word 'socialist' was first used in 1827 in the Owenite *Co-operative Magazine* as a general description of Robert Owen's cooperative doctrines, and then as '*socialisme*' in 1832 in *La Globe*, the journal of the followers of Claude-Henri de Rouvroy, Comte de Saint-Simon (1760–1825). The ideas of these men were very different. But the general connotation of the word in the 1830s was something like this: an invented system of society that stressed the social as against the selfish, the cooperative as against the competitive, sociability as against individual self-sufficiency and self-interest; strict social controls on the accumulation and use of private property; and either economic equality or at least rewards according to merits (merits judged socially), or (a middle position) rewards judged according to need.

Socialism went beyond even radical democracy. There was no socialism in Tom Paine, for instance. The largest popular movements in both Britain and France stood for reform of the franchise, for a democratic or a more democratic system, but within the context of the new economic liberties, a market not a guided economy. Few Chartists, for instance, were socialists in any real sense, even though their fullest programme, *Propositions of the National Reform League* (1850), borrowed some socialist ideas about public provision of work and prevention of poverty. But the whole tone and temper of Chartism was of radical democracy, a belief that reform of the electoral system, free provision of education and of small holdings for the unemployed poor would solve all social problems and render individual economic competition fair. It was far closer to American Jacksonian democracy than to anything sensibly called 'socialist'. Certainly they were egalitarian and anti-aristocratic but their ethic was that of 'independency', a market society for small men and small proprietors, not the fraternity of communal life and production: they had no vision that to get justice it was necessary to reshape the economic system as thoroughly as they wished to reform the political system.

Early socialism was a minority reaction to the practice of capitalist ethics and to an increasingly industrial society. It sought some middle way between concepts of 'status' and concepts of 'contract' through which the worth of all individuals could be defined, protected and nurtured. Its influence at the time was small but its influence later was great. Doctrines of agrarian socialism emerged quite early but it is important to see that the origins of socialism lay in the perception that there were unique problems in the new capitalist, urban industrial order.

The French Revolution was egalitarian in spirit but the means it adopted were mainly negative. It had been more concerned to remove restraints on trade and the accumulation and use of property, typical of the mercantilist system of the old regime, than to impose controls on property, still less to implement schemes of confiscation or compulsory levelling (which in fact were not typical of early socialisms). But socialism was nothing if it was not a critique of the emerging new capitalism and an account of *how* (unlike utopianism) to achieve a better, alternative social order. The specification was a stiff one. For the intellectual power and the literary prestige of the Scottish and English *laissez-faire* economists was formidable. Early socialism grew as a popular movement. Early socialism had its would-be rivals to Adam Smith,

Edmund Burke, Malthus and Ricardo in Saint-Simon, Fourier and then Proudhon (1809–65), and many minor figures; but until Marx there were no general theorists of the stature of the liberal economists.

The socialists differed from the utopians less in their long-term values than in their determination to offer a realistic and plausible account of how to get from unhappy here to felicitous there. The heroes of most utopias either dream or wake up in the future. But realism can be highly relative, especially to men full both of intense rage at the poverty and injustice of the present and of noble visions of the future. Early socialism was often tinged with crankery. Fourier had the simplest methodology: he advertised in the newspapers for a philanthropist to finance his *phalansteres* and for many years waited in a café at the same time each day for him to come. But that was hardly less utopian than the 'sleeper awakes' school of fiction. Most histories of socialism have been filled with names of original or eccentric people whose books and pamphlets sadly have had no known influence on any group or movement. Even anti-traditionalists are at times avid for ancestors. But there are some figures among the early socialists who both had some influence in their time and who expressed some ideas of lasting importance. Most early socialists put their entire faith in persuasion, whether exercised through representative institutions in the existing state or through setting up cooperative institutions as a noble example outside the conventional legal order of state power — sometimes literally outside, as some Owenites and Fourierists moved heroically but vainly into the American wilderness, the attempted 'prairie utopias'. Few of the early socialists believed that insurrection was the path. It was widely believed that one of the 'lessons' of the French Revolution had been that that path had failed: violent revolution was doomed to devour its own children. And few had any faith that the old order would somehow simply collapse.

The origins of socialism and those of sociology are very close to each other. They both arose from the shattering of the old order and the aroused climate of expectations in the revolution. Talking at table one day in 1803, with every word being recorded, Napoleon declared that 'the metaphysicians are my pet aversion':

I have classified all these people under the head of ideologists, which,
by the way, is peculiarly and literally suited to them: *idea seekers* —
hollow ideas as a rule. Now the application of the term ideologist to
that class has cast even more ridicule upon them than I dared expect.
The expression stuck, I think because it came from me. . . . those
poor scholars [*savants*] don't understand themselves. How could I
come to terms with them to govern the way they think I ought to? Yes,
they have a craze for interfering with my policies. They talk, talk,
talk. My aversion to this breed of ideologists goes to the point of
hatred.

One of these ideas-mongers who angered him must have been
Saint-Simon, perhaps especially because Saint-Simon in his
first works cast Napoleon himself in the role of the enlightened
Prince or 'Great Legislator' who would implement Saint-
Simon's new discovery of a science of society.

Saint-Simon came from an impoverished junior branch of a
great aristocratic family but he fought in the American War of
Independence and supported the French Revolution. He
became convinced that mankind had reached the third and
greatest turning point in the history of man, the revolution
being a result of this crisis, not, in itself, the driving force.
History moved between long 'organic' periods, when technology and social order were in harmony, and periods of crisis
and disequilibrium when new technology was emerging but
being resisted by the values and customs of the old organic
order. The new technology was industry and the new values
scientific. The new century, the nineteenth-century, would be
the era of science and industry from which human unity and
universal prosperity would follow. Precisely how this was to
happen was to be the urgent study of *les savants* organized
into great Academies. Napoleon had already established an
Academy of Natural Sciences to which was to be added an
Academy of Social Scientists and an Academy of Artists.
Saint-Simon reclassified *les lumiéres* from time to time, but
his essential idea was always that government should be con-
ducted and society reconstructed according to the advice of
'luminaries' — a specialized learned elite. 'All social institutions should have as their aim', said the legend at the head of
La Globe, 'the moral, intellectual and physical improvement
of the poorest and most numerous class.' (Actually, at the
time he wrote '*la classe la plus nombreuse et la plus pauvre*'

were peasants not city workers; that he virtually ignored them showed how much the new socialists looked to the future, believing not merely in progress but that they could foretell its course.)

These learned elites, *les savants*, had the duty of working for the general prosperity of society. The state had an obligation to find work for all its inhabitants and all its inhabitants had an obligation to labour for the common good. The idea was neither democratic nor intended to be egalitarian. Rewards should be distributed and wages alloted to each according to one's *capacity* to work for the common good. Everyone was equally capable of some socially useful work. There was only room for one social class in society, though rewards would vary within it: *les industriels* who comprised both labourers and entrepreneurs, as contrasted to those he bluntly called *les oisifs*, the idle or the layabouts, especially the idle rich.

Le savants would have control of a compulsory educational system, primary as well as secondary, which would indoctrinate (he used the word openly) the true principles of a scientific industrial culture. Administration would be through three chambers: one of engineers and artists (by which he meant creative thinkers of all kinds) to formulate plans; a second of scientists with the duty of appraising the feasibility of these plans; and a third of industrialists and bankers charged with their implementation. And, for fair measure, he supplied in his last writings a 'New Christianity' (quite unlike the old one) which was to be the compulsory social ethic of consensus and harmony. He seemed to have little concern for either democracy or civil liberties. By some definitions this is hardly even a type of socialism, not even bad socialism. But such definitions would be too ideal. His picture of an essential harmony between capital and labour might not be socialist, but it is also a vision of a centralized and planned industrial society administered for the common good and looking to the future. It is, in a sense, a picture of a capitalist society without a free-market but with a collective capacity to organize and steer the economy for the common good. Doctrines as different as the Fabianism of the Webbs and Stalin's coarse and cruel version of Communism ('state capitalism'?) each owe something to Saint-Simon. And the theory underlying it all is of stages of human

history, even if not in terms of class struggle but of techno-
logical invention. (And all this was argued with such a vast
erudition that it earned praise from both Hegel and Engels,
although they each disagreed profoundly with most of his
analysis and all his conclusions.)

As Rousseau was to become more revolutionary after his
death, so Saint-Simon became more a socialist. His disciples
both venerated him and reinterpreted him, a not uncommon
fate of prophets. Under the editorship of Saint-Amand
Bazard his grieving disciples quickly produced *La Doctrine
saint-simonienne*, a short restatement which moved further
than he had ever done towards a kind of 'state socialism'. The
crucial reinterpretation was to declare that any inheritance of
wealth was incompatible with his principles. (Perhaps, yet he
had always avoided this question.) Their veneration, however,
was all too literal. He himself had become aware that his
unrivalled grasp of both the past and the future course of
human history must have been divinely inspired. His disciples
not merely venerated him as a modern saint but saw him as the
founder of a new religion. And like so many new religions and
future socialist societies and parties, they immediately split.
The first great schism was largely between the political wing,
headed by Bazard, and the religious wing, inspired and led to a
pyrrhic victory by Barthelemy-Prosper Enfantin — an extraordinary character who in searching for civil engineering
projects to cement a mystic marriage between East and West
was to make the first plans for the Suez Canal, though he was
elbowed out by a fellow Saint-Simonian and graduate of the
Ecole Polytechnique, Ferdinand de Lesseps. The idea of
socialist engineers is now very strange and distant, let alone
that engineering should be a specifically socialist discipline
and vocation (yet H.G. Wells and George Bernard Shaw were
Saint-Simonians at least in this).

A very different tradition of socialism stemmed from
Fourier. From a merchant family, impoverished in the revolution, he earned his living variously as a clerk, a printer, a
commercial traveller, was largely self-taught and until the last
ten years of his life could only pursue his studies and writing
for a few hours each night. Yet he had a broad and popular
vision of a new social system and also composed many huge,
visionary, detailed and ridiculous cosmologies. He is the

paradigm case of the crazy autodidact. Cole wrote that 'There is much in Fourier that is fantastic — in his latest writings much that is plainly mad. It is unnecessary to dwell on the fantasies, which have no connection with the essence of his teaching.'

His broad vision was that work could be *pleasant* and adjusted to the *character* and *wishes* of each *individual*, not just socially beneficial. We are most likely to find work pleasant when it is varied, when it is cooperative, and when we can make things well crafted and to last: a pleasure to look upon and a pleasure to make, and to make them as a whole — he bitterly opposed accepting the division of labour as the great principle of social organization. Like Schiller, he thought that Adam Smith's pin factory, where each does part of a carefully divided task with unprecendented efficiency, was less a boon to mankind than a threat to human nature; it would alienate man from nature. Families should live together in communities small enough for each to know each other, large enough to be reasonably self-sufficient and to allow her a diversity of talent. Whereas Saint-Simon thought in terms of science, industry and central administration, Fourier wished to prevent the spread of the industrial principle which he thought threatened sociability, true individuality and pleasure in work. He turned his back, as it were, on Newton, Adam Smith and Arkwright. Men should live and work in the countryside or, if necessary, in small workshops in small towns.

Saint-Simon's ideas appealed, not surprisingly, to the graduates of the *Ecole Polytechnique* and Fourier's appealed more to self-taught craftsmen and tradesmen who felt threatened by large-scale enterprises and the division of labour. He took much from Rousseau including a belief that the common man (honest and natural) was more virtuous than either the aristocrat (sophisticated and corrupt) or the scholar (artificial and arrogant). The common man must not merely be able to turn his hand to anything, which was very much the American Jeffersonian and Jacksonian ideal, or the Scottish 'lad o' pairts', but must in fact do so. Society should be reconstructed to ensure this.

It would be reconstructed in cooperative *phalansteres* of 1,600 persons cultivating about 5,000 acres. Each would have common buildings with common services, including restaurants, crèches and recreation rooms, but the brothers and sisters could also have apartments of their own and would somehow move back and forth according to taste. He was not a literal egalitarian. Basic needs would be well provided for and extravagance and ostentation would be outlawed by public opinion; but each person or family could invest more or less of their wages in the share-capital of each community and receive interest. Thus special skills and special effort should be rewarded, and families were to be free to buy different sorts of apartment and furniture etcetera. There would be a minimum and a maximum defined not *a priori* but by the good sense, general will or civic spirit of each community collectively.

He grew more and more fantastical in suggesting elaborate rules for the *phalansteres*. But when his ideas, late in his life, began to attract attention, most people ignored the specificity of his fantasies, or substituted their own. To his annoyance his tortuous specifications were derided or ignored but his general principle, which he variously called 'harmony', 'solidarity', *Unitéism, Collectisme, Sociantisme or Mutualisme*, was treated respectfully by some but simply taken over by many more at second-hand. His essential points were taken to be his anti-industrial spirit, the cooperative mode of production and a benign ambiguity about whether his communities were simply turning their back on the state and conventional society, or whether they would be so much more attractive — even efficient, he sometimes convinced himself — that they would gradually and peaceably replace the urban capitalist mode of production. If so, they would then be loosely linked in, first, huge national confederations, then European, finally global. But even if a cooperative federation did not emerge, the way of life on a commune was better, richer and more satisfying for those good souls who dared and could.

This was the true beginning of communitarian socialism. And for all its seeming hopelessness, for all its perpetually attendant eccentricities and crankeries, the idea was a standing reproof to the autocratic and bureaucratic excesses of the centralists; and it was an image of a way of life at least magnetic enough to pull many of us away from serving the state to serving the community — or rather 'communities'. Put in more abstract terms, here is the beginning of a pluralistic theory and doctrine of power rather than, in their eyes, the

almost equal obsession of Hobbists, Leninists and Fabians
with the central state.

The case was strongest, moreover, when it talked of the
quality of life rather than production and the economy.
Fourierism was widely preached in the United States. His leading American disciple, Albert Brisbane, published a sensible
summary of his teachings in 1840 significantly called (in a
country of intense and explicit individualism), *The Social
Destiny of Man*. And working communities were attempted in
America — more so than in France or Britain. Hawthorne's
novel, *Blithdale Romance*, described the Brook Farm Community of 1832, founded by a group of New England intellectuals including Margaret Fuller and extolled by Emerson. None
of these 'noble experiments' lasted long. Perhaps the self-
imposed disciplines are too harsh when we enter a tight and
deliberately isolated community in hope of a more satisfying
way of secular life, and not for the all-consuming love or fear
of God. Certainly the religious communities tended to last
longer. And if communities were not tightly conformist and
geographically isolated, then it was all too easy simply to give
up and walk out at the first or second set of real difficulties.
Communities founded on invented secular ideologies seem
prone to schism when each individual can reinterpret the
ideology. But in Professor Arthur Bestor's modern study,
Backwoods Utopias, as in C. Nordhoff's classic *Communistic
Societies of the United States* (1875), more trivial reasons
are revealed as most often leading to breakdown: under-
capitalization, incompetent financial management, and an
excess of over-argumentative and work-shy, or simply incompetent, intellectuals, too often helpless without servants.

Fourier provided inspiration for the anarchist tradition of
socialism — the noble example of the common people (more
often the craftsman, in fact) engaged in honest toil, whereas
Saint-Simon pointed towards state planning through the
permeation and persuasion of a dedicated scientific elite. Both
of them thought of revolution as a long drawn-out process
through time (if Saint-Simon thought of revolution at all,
through his followers certainly did). There was, however, also
an insurrectionary revolutionary socialist tradition of 'red
republicans' who held that the Jacobins had been right not to
flinch at violent seizure of power, purges and the salutary

terror; but that they had had inadequate or self-defeating economic objectives. Louis-August Blanqui (1805–61) was the embodiment and would-be leader of all such hard, brave and fanatic men, the past-master and living martyr of the hopeless rising. Thirty-three of his seventy-six years were spent in prison, yet he died of a stroke on a political platform not on a guillotine. He and such men looked back to Babeuf and the famous but hopeless 'conspiracy of equals'; indeed they were generally known as '*babouvistes*'.

Blanqui was no theorist but his doctrines were clear and notorious. He believed that a small, resolute and highly disciplined party could seize the state apparatus by force. (He only ever got the size and the resolution right.) Once in power a mass movement could be created by control and use of popular education; and this power would be used to impose a strictly egalitarian social order of common ownership which he termed 'Communism'. He thought the word 'socialist' was tainted with soft and silly Fourierist hopes that the lion would lie down with the lamb if spoken to nicely, the capitalist with the worker. In imitation of Babeuf, he called himself a 'proletarian' — a word hitherto unused since Roman times. It smacked of class war to those with even a little learning. But the class needed leadership by professional revolutionaries. Spontaneous popular risings rarely occurred and when they did they were, if without such leaders, put down easily.

After the *coup d'état* or seizure of power could come the revolution. What precisely would happen afterwards? He thought it foolish to predict. Revolutionaries must be tactically flexible. They must seize power by any means and impose what he christened 'a dictatorship of the proletariat' (a splendid and frightening paradox) to eradicate the last vestiges of the old order. Now the word 'dictatorship' connoted, to anyone in the least familiar with Roman history, an officer given absolute power legally by the Senate for the duration of an emergency, authorized to act as ruthlessly and arbitrarily as necessary to save or regenerate the republic. Some time after the elimination of the old order there would emerge, he definitely if somewhat vaguely envisaged, a system of self-governing *communes* which would, in time replace the state apparatus. And '*commune*' in French has, after all, the double meaning of the smallest unit of local government and of

'community' as a deeply-felt social bonding, whether func-
tional or geographical.

All this sounds very Marxist, except that Marx believed that
a revolution could only take place when the fundamental
social structure of the old regime was already in crisis, and that
one sign of a revolutionary situation would be the emergence
of a mass working class movement. He mocked Blanqui's
'putschism' as impossibly voluntaristic and opportunistic, as
just a blind anger and an outraged sense of justice undirected
by any clear understanding of history or economic development. Lenin shared Marx's mockery for such men, but ended
up successful in 1917 in a situation much closer to Blanqui's
vision than to Marx's, and either the will to exercise dictatorship or the emergency then proved not to be temporary.

Pierre-Joseph Proudhon (1809–65) stands out among the
early socialists as the virtual founder of both the important
traditions of socialism that have been Marxism's main intellectual and political rivals. Fourierism and Saint-Simonianism
are tendencies that influence the socialist tradition but neither
constituted movements. But *anarchism* and *democratic
socialism* are each self-renewing movements, taking on a life
of their own quite independent of the Master and his more
inflexible disciples.

How could somebody be read as stating both the plausibility
of anarchism and of democratic socialism? Partly this arose
from the shrewdness, brilliance, persistence and sheer number
of his polemics, both as a journalist and as a writer of books,
against the existing state power. So specific were his targets, as
a reactive quite as much as a systematic writer, that it was easy
to think that he was really advocating a better and a juster
form of state, rather than using abuses of state power as living
symbols of the inherent injustice of any centralized state
power.

But there was a deeper reason. For Proudhon everything
began and ended with *liberty*, and with the liberty of ordinary
people, not just of the intellectuals, to do as they pleased so
long as they did no harm to others. Ordinary people, who like
himself had grown up in poverty, are restrained in their capacity to exercise liberty by inequality, economic exploitation,
and direct government censorship and oppression. Remove
these things and men and women can be free. Liberty is not

imposing a particular reformed social order. Liberty is the absence of those conditions that prevent me from becoming myself at my best. And it is the state that embodies or enforces all these obstacles, whether as government of the few or exercised in the name of a majority. He made use of the Greek term 'anarchy' which hitherto had either meant simply the absence of government, or else negatively disorder.

> The ideal republic is positive anarchy. It is neither liberty subordinated to order, as in a constitutional monarchy, nor liberty imprisoned in order. It is liberty free from all its shackles, superstitions, sophistries, usury, authority: it is reciprocal liberty, not limited liberty; liberty is not the daughter but the mother of order.

Some 'positive' disorder prevents the growth of uniformity in human society, some 'contradictions' can make for variety and stimulate originality in human character. True order will be egalitarian but lively. In the absence of hierarchy there will be more character not less.

Property, he famously said, was theft; but he meant the accumulation of property based on interest, rent and the stealing of the 'surplus value' of the labour that people put into making things. He did not mean personal property, used by and in families for their own use, if it was acquired by people's own labour. So once again, here was another socialist who did not even claim to believe in literal economic equality (the perennial caricature, and the perennial impossibilist deviation), but rather in an egalitarian ethos. For this reason he attacked both the Saint-Simonians and the Fourierists. He thought the former elitist, entirely concerned with knowledge and philanthropy, unconcerned with liberty and humanity as ends in themselves; and he thought the latter were likely to create a series of rustic authoritarian hells rather than freely cooperative communities. It would be no advance to substitute the tyranny of a local majority for that of the state.

Greater economic equality was desired by Proudhon for the sake of individual liberty, and for that reason alone. He believed in a classless society of all workers and not in class war as the mechanism of social change. Social change could only come from the voluntary agreement of ordinary working people. He had contempt for the concealed elitism of the proletarian *Babouvistes*. When he met Marx, who at first admired him for critiques of Saint-Simon and Fourier and sought to educate him in Hegel and dialectical thinking, Proudhon soon recognized a latent authoritarianism both in his personality and in some of his key ideas. 'Do not let us become the leaders of a new intolerance', he wrote to Marx in 1846, 'let us gather in to ourselves and encourage protest against our own ideas', a prescient reproof that led to an abrupt and angry rupture. By 1864 when the International Workingmen's Association (the First International) was founded, it was Proudhon's followers who were Marx's strongest opponents. In response to Proudhon's book of 1846, *System of Economic Contradictions* (which had the subtitle 'or the Philosophy of Poverty') Marx wrote in the following year his famous polemic, *The Poverty of Philosophy*.

All was not quite as it seemed, however, when Proudhon called himself an anarchist and argued for an extreme egalitarian individualism equally opposed to the State and to 'associations'. For there should be free credit available for all worthy small enterprises, or rather for banks to charge no more by way of interest than to meet the costs of the bank and of the administration of the law. For there was to be a consti-tutional structure of public law to deal with disputes between individuals and to achieve an orderly organization of work and exchange of produce and services, indeed to constitute and control the banks. 'Constituent assemblies' would be summoned to create such laws, would not stay around but would be resummoned if need arose to reform them. The difference between frequent (anarchist) constituent assemblies and infrequent (bourgeois) parliaments or assemblies could prove a fine one. Proudhon was in danger of reinventing the wheel, though giving it a nicer name. But formally he was committed to the view that even the most representative and democratic parliament was simply another form of or disguise for the oppressive state.

Anarchists were to split fine hairs happily with the master over the years, or more typically were to lapse back into Fourierist beliefs in communes as small, self-governing cooperative communities, although some anarchists delibe-rately cultivated small, skilled and solitary trades where the division of labour was irrelevant, like cobbling or clock-making and repairing. They waited peacefully for the state to collapse out of its great weight (both Proudhon and Marx had strong if rival lines in 'inevitable contradictions').

Some socialists, however, were more urban and urbane than the Fourierists, more democratic than the Saint-Simonians and the Comteans, and also evolutionary rather than insurrectionary. They took all of the libertarian passages to heart in Proudhon's writings and then either exaggerated greatly the limited role he gave to constituent assemblies, or else ignored his institutional thinking entirely. So he became part of the Pantheon of French Socialists, in the late nineteenth and early twentieth century sense: that is, not Communists or rigid Marxists, but democratic Socialists. His own anarchism was easily watered down to arguments in favour of decentralism, never easy arguments to sustain in France where an extraordinary sense of 'the State' as the embodiment of the nation, the lasting legacy of Napoleon, has normally dominated both Left and Right. But not always. Perhaps it was the very strength of this tradition that drove Proudhon into anarchism. Sometimes, even unconsciously, you have to exaggerate to reach a more moderate position. It depends what you are attacking. And our own behaviour can be much affected by that of our opponents.

No possible socialism, let alone early socialism, stands on its own in solemn isolation. Socialism's strength and *raison d'être* was as a critique of urban capitalism, not as an abstract utopian fantasy of a return to Eden. The New Jerusalem would have to be built upon the 'dark Satanic mills' not on virgin land in the wilderness.

Robert Owen (1771–1857) saw industry and the factory as the liberators of mankind from poverty and ignorance, but better and more free if reorganized on cooperative principles. Owen was a self-made cotton manufacturer who in 1799 had bought a controlling interest in the New Lanark Mills in Scotland which he then ran on enlightened if paternalistic and strictly supervised lines. The mills were run as a closed community with improved housing, sanitation, laundries, regulated shops and free and compulsory schools. This 'model factory' might later degenerate into 'the company town' but Owen and his Quaker partners provided these comprehensive services to ensure the health, contentment and education of their workers, not to exploit them. His original New Lanark practices were not cooperative at all, in any sense of worker control or voluntary participation: New Lanark was an enlightened paternalism which seemed to prove the point that if a manufacturer treated his workers more or less as equal human beings, they responded in the efficiency of their work. And he set a standard of comprehensive welfare provision quite unknown to charitable institutions and philanthropies of the time: the memory of New Lanark became the root of municipal socialism in the last quarter of the century and the basis of much of the early thinking about a welfare state.

His *New View of Society* of 1813 and his *Address to the Inhabitants of New Lanark* of 1816 recounted how all this could be done while still making a profit, and contained an attack on the new factory system. He denounced it because of bad physical conditions and bad moral conditions — especially touching the employment of young children; and for teaching by example the crudest, most selfish and most materialistic competitive struggle for existence. This happened both by the general refusal to spend anything on the comfort, health or safety of workers that diminished profit and by the specific system of encouraging competitive piece-work rather than paying a fair wage for a fair day's work. The environment created by the new factories was, Owen argued, debasing human character. Human character, he held, was largely formed by environment — a view which at the time was not merely novel, but could be construed as irreligious. A better environment, which could be provided, as at New Lanark, would create not merely happier but better people. And education, both of children and adults, was the most powerful conditioning factor of all.

Owen soon broadened his advocacy to urge the establish-ment by public authorities of 'Villages of Cooperation' to put paupers and unemployed to work, but now not to be supervised in detail but financed to try to support and better themselves collectively. Some hard-headed authorities wondered if this might not be an alternative to paying for paupers' Workhouses out of the rates. But he was soon advocating not merely a 'right to work' but also arguing that cooperation was itself an educa-tive and morally improving process, perhaps even superior to the new virtue of individual competition. There was enough revulsion at the harshness of conditions in the new factories, and also worry about unrest among city workers and the unemployed, to lead for a while, in both Parliament and polite society, to a considerable interest in Owen's ideas and practices.

The old landed ruling class had, in the early nineteenth-century, little love for the new manufacturers and self-made entrepreneurs. The gentry idealized the paternal care they showed for their rural tenants, or argued only from the best examples; but some had a genuine perception of and revulsion from the dehumanizing routines, the soul-destroying drudgery and the anonymity of the new factories. And 'property' was still perceived basically as land and not the business share. Owen was asked to London to give evidence to two Select Committees of Parliament dealing with the Poor Laws and with proposals for Factory Acts. And he lectured widely. At first his proposals were taken seriously. Bankers and Royal Dukes met him and gave him a sympathetic hearing.

For a moment it seemed as if Robert Owen might be taken up as a cult or fashion in the drawing rooms of those of the English aristocracy who liked to patronize literature and learning, just as Rousseau had been in the salons of the French aristocracy. But like Rousseau, his ideas developed too rapidly and were too serious for comfort. It became apparent from his lectures that he believed in a completely secular, non-religious universal system of free education and that the cooperative mode of production he had urged for paupers could, indeed more and more he argued should, be applied to all industry and involve a thorough-going reformation of society. As his eyes were set on this world and not the next, he seemed worse than a Methodist. The establishment's interest in his proposals came to an abrupt end and he became more and more extreme in his advocacy of cooperative production.

Owen addressed 'Memorials' to the Heads of State of Europe gathered at the Aix-la-Chapelle Conference in 1817, arguing that an 'age of plenty' could emerge for all mankind if his new principles were applied both to the creation of wealth and to its use. And he went there to try to lobby them. The calm businessman had become the passionate enthusiast. He became convinced that the cooperative mode of production would replace capitalism if only a few cooperative communities could be established to point the way, to be a beacon light of practicality and example.

He hoped for better support in the United States, where he carried his message in 1824 and was invited to address Congress. The invitation was based on a misunderstanding. The Congressmen and Senators quickly realized that he had moved beyond, too far beyond, the practical man's view of New Lanark — being nice to the workers and keeping them hard-working and quiet. But there was little hostility to or sense of threat from his 'cooperative socialism' — a somewhat impractical but nice enough way of life for those who liked such a way of life. He purchased 20,000 acres of land to found and name New Harmony. He would direct it in its early years and then turn it over to the democratic administration of the settlers. Unfortunately few of the settlers seemed to have the qualities he wanted for such a venture, though some did to excess. After three years of frustration and argument he left them as a very loose federation of squabbling small groups. New Harmony failed for much the same mixture of mundane reasons as did the Fourierist settlements. Virtually ruined, Owen returned to Britain.

His ideas, however, had caught on among many working people in Britain. When he left for America they asked why they should not try some of his ideas for themselves. Producer cooperatives as a rule fared badly but many small consumer cooperatives lasted and soon formed large federations. From 1831 regular congresses of cooperatives were held and many journals were launched to popularize their ideas and to instruct their members. And 'New Lanark', more in myth than in its over-regulated, dour reality, became an inspiring example of what services towns could offer their inhabitants. Moreover Owen himself had both come round to this viewpoint and found a new cause and career, even more explicitly socialist. He attempted to organize nationally the many small trade unions that came into existence, or emerged above ground, after 1824 when Parliament repealed the Combination Acts of 1799 and 1800 which had prohibited unions. He tried to establish 'A Grand National Moral Union of the Productive Classes' which would introduce a new social order of cooperative production simply by refusing to continue working under the capitalist system. It never grew large enough; and most trade unionists, then and now, were more concerned with wage negotiations and immediate conditions of work.

The Grand National Union, of which Owen was for a while President, fell apart in the fear that followed the famous prosecution and transportation in 1834 of the six Dorchester labourers ('the Tolpuddle martyrs') on the trumped-up charge of administering illegal oaths, since trade unions as such and even strikes were not illegal. But the repression was itself a sign that the new movements were feared. Both cooperative societies and trade unions grew greatly in numbers. All had immediate objectives; some were strongly for social transformation, all had some sympathies with such ideas, and nearly all saw social transformation as being obtainable, perhaps only obtainable, peaceably, patiently and yet persistently through industrial more than political action. Trade unions and cooperative societies were then more important engines of social change than political parties.

4

Marx and Marxism: Theory and Practice

Theory

When towards the end of his life Karl Marx (1818–83) read some of the writings of French disciples, he growled that he had never himself been a Marxist. For the problem had begun even in his lifetime. Engels mocked the way Russian disciples 'interpret passages . . . in the most contradictory ways, just as if they were texts from the classics or the New Testament'. Marx bitterly rebuked his young English disciple, H.M. Hyndman for his *England For All*, one of the best popular accounts of Marx's doctrines ever written. His rage at plagiarism (Hyndman naively explained to Marx that 'your name is so much detested here' that he had not mentioned it) was matched by his prejudice that it must be 'vulgarisation' and 'gross simplification'. Indeed, it is very difficult to retrieve Marx from Marxism, our minds are so overlaid with so many subsequent interpretations of apparent scholarly or obviously political authority; and also with popular traditions of Marxism whose sources are almost entirely word of mouth — like the Militant faction today; or if based on the written word at all, then on tendentious sectarian handbooks.

The sense in which modern intellectuals like Althusser and Poulantzas, who cannot write one sentence that would be either intelligible to a worker or acceptable to Marx, and in which Hyndman, Lenin, Rosa Luxembourg, Stalin, Laski, Mao Tse Tung, Castro and Gorbachev are all not merely Marxists, but can often claim to be authoritative expounders of a living doctrine, is, indeed, very strange and strained. But no more strange than to think that the Pope, the Bishop of Durham, Mr Billy Graham and Dr Ian Paisley are all Christian ministers. The main difference is that the world-wide diffusion and dilution of Marx's ideas happened far more quickly than those of Christ's. 'Dilution' is a technical term in the history of ideas, it means change but not necessarily weakening, sometimes a strengthening of the original spirit. The problem of interpretation, in both the ideology and the religion, is compounded by each big disciple not merely claiming that theirs is the one true reading of the Word but that the Word is the only Word, that there is no salvation or true morality even outside the Church and no true socialism save Marxism. At least it is clear that the latter proposition is untrue. It would be far too simple, however, to say that Marx is no more to blame for Stalin than Rousseau for Robespierre. For part of the problem is that while Marx preached the unity of theory and practice, he never, through the vast body of his writings, set out any complete and fully consistent, still less a final, statement of his thought. *Das Kapital* was unfinished. The *Anti-Dühring* is a clear exposition of Marxism but it is by Engels, and Engels was more systematic but also more dogmatic than Marx.

The shortest but most famous of his writings, *The Communist Manifesto*, is still both the most comprehensive statement of a general theory, and the most influential. The vast body of his writings (forty-one volumes in the modern German collected edition) were mainly occasional pieces, journalism and letters; always remembering that letters from philosophers or statemen were often premeditated and considered statements, written in full consciousness that they would be passed around, copied, read to meetings and congresses, printed in friendly newspapers. And some of his writings, let alone notebooks and drafts, were never published in his lifetime. Twenty years ago a 'young Marx' was discovered who seemed to Western Marxists of a liberal disposition to be more humanistic than the older Marx. Debate rages as to whether he, or they, ever grew up. Sometimes he planned works slowly and carefully, sometimes he dashed them off with speed and anger; and it is not always the long-wrought works that have worn best. Small wonder that all the rival schools of Marxism can, at their best, look so scholarly, and can each find textual authority for 'the essential Marx' on whom they build their differences.

Some try to distinguish levels of abstraction: there is Marx the philosopher talking of general truths, the vast impersonal laws or tendencies that give unintended consequences to the multiplicity of human actions; and there is Marx the historian, more often the journalist indeed, giving a brilliant account of an actual contemporary political situation, full of accidents, events, personalities, skill, will and free actions. To the philosophic Marx, politics itself was just part of the super-structure of society, a result, not a cause, of social and eco-nomic change; indeed, more specifically, politics was a device used by the bourgeoisie in the leisure they purchase from the expropriated surplus-value of the labour of the masses in order to try to prevent any further revolution. Their own replacement of the feudal aristocracy heralded an age of per-petual peace and free trade. But Marx the contemporary histo-rian and journalist, indeed Marx the would-be master tacti-cian of the proletarian movement, had a sharp sense of how much political will, skill or incompetence can shape, not just transitory events, but more lasting social conditions. Marx himself did not observe such distinctions, moved from high theory to low politics in a sentence — as so often in *The Com-munist Manifesto*. Engels was more self-conscious of and careful about the distinction between philosophy and political polemic, but then he is accused, for his pains, of creating an image of a Marx who was a determinist, who was for ever saying that this or that must 'necessarily' be so or will 'inevitably' come to pass. Yet Engels may only have been deliberately presenting Marx's Marxism at the highest possible level of abstraction and generality, knowing quite well that in every concrete situation and nation the colour, shape and tex-ture of the garments men and women wear will differ but not their basic drives and needs.

There is growing agreement among scholars that while Marx was the greatest and most comprehensive of socialist thinkers, the most original and the most suggestive, he was a good deal less systematic and consistent than once supposed. He has lately even been praised for being speculative more than systematic (as could never have been said to his face). Marx needs rescuing from Marxists; but their error is not in getting him wrong but in supposing that there is a completely, self-contained, coherent and comprehensive system of theory from which necessary inferences can be drawn for policy and action. At his best, he made no such claims himself; at his worst, he did; and the confusion is made worse by a biographical or psychological factor: he was vain and intellectually intolerant, he would accuse people of deserting socialism if they criticized him in any way, failed to take his advice or to lend him money. Pinpricks provoked thunderbolts and he threw the book at critics — or rather the imagined book that was always in his mind's eye and gnawing at his guts to be finished. He left a deadly legacy to Marxist socialists of melodramatic polemic rather than of measured reasoning.

Some try to distinguish the structure of his thought from both the content and the polemical excesses, by saying that they adopt Marxism as a *method* but not as a dogma nor as a direct guide to policy. The method suggests what empirical questions to ask and it defines the limits of human action, it sets parameters but not directions. There is obvious sense in this. To accuse present-day Marxists of the kind of Tom Bottomore, Eric Hobsbawm or Ralph Miliband of all the sins of the father, and of his squabbling and violent children, is absurd. But this only shifts the problem, even if to a more reasonable and less grandiloquent level. For we must then ask, what *was* Marx's method? And then new fighting breaks out: to some his method is basically economic, to others sociological or to others historical. And then, of course, to free oneself from the assumptions of Marx's own time, which not even Marx himself could do according to his own theory, Marxism must become, it is said, 'a living method', capable of change.

Many modern Marxists are clearly in a Marxist tradition but freely use methods from other traditions for particular problems and may reach a wide range of agreement on policy with other socialists. At this point 'Marxism' ceases to have an exclusive meaning, such as Marx plainly wanted, and it hardly matters if writers call themselves Marxists or not. Yet no kind of socialist can now be unaffected by Marx's achievement. What basically was 'Marxism', the popular theory and doctrine that can be located in Marx's own writings and is not actually contradicted by anything he said?

The doctrine was always, and still is, best expressed in *The Communist Manifesto* of 1848. A critic of Marxism, Isaiah Berlin, called it 'very nearly a work of genius':

No other political movement or cause can claim to have produced anything comparable with it in eloquence or power. It is a document of prodigious dramatic force; in form it is an edifice of bold and arresting historical generalisations, mounting to a denunciation of the existing order in the name of the avenging forces of the future, much of it written in prose which has the lyrical quality of a great revolutionary hymn . . .

[Berlin, Karl Marx, 2nd edn (1948), p. 150]

And Engels, in the Preface to the English edition of 1888, repeated what he had said in the German edition of 1883, in the year of Marx's death, that there was a 'fundamental proposition' that belonged to Marx alone. Surely this proposition is the basis of Marxism as a popular doctrine:

. . . .that in every historical epoch, the prevailing mode of economic production and exchange, and the social organisation necessarily following from it, form the basis from which is built up, and from which alone can be explained, the political and intellectual history of that epoch; that consequently the whole history of mankind (since the dissolution of primitive tribal society, holding land in common ownership) has been a history of class struggles, contests between exploiting and exploited, ruling and oppressed classes; that the history of these class struggles forms a series of evolutions in which, nowadays, a stage has been reached where the exploited and oppressed class — the proletariat — cannot obtain its emancipation from the sway of the exploiting and ruling class — the bourgeoisie — without at the same time, and once and for all, emancipating society at large from all exploitation, oppression, class distinctions and class struggles.

And he added that 'this proposition . . . is destined to do for history what Darwin's theory has done for biology'.

So Marx attacks the followers of Fourier, Proudhon and Owen: the emancipation of the working class depends on struggle, not on Rousseauistic good will. He labels cooperative, communal, and decentralized socialist ideas 'utopian'. This was not to dismiss them entirely but to signpost them towards the future in a classless society where the state has lost its oppressive character: such ideas may be goals, they cannot be the present means. An American journalist, of an older generation, once asked Marx what he thought was the ultimate form of 'being' or of the philosophical question, 'what is?'; Marx replied '*struggle*'. And a playful questionnaire from his young daughter brought these responses: 'Your idea of happiness?' '*To fight.*' 'The vice you most detest?' '*Servility.*'

He rounded on Saint-Simon with greater vehemence: the proletariat must emancipate themselves. If an educated elite, however devoted and scientific, try to do it for them, they will become a new ruling class. Yet he shares Saint-Simon's belief, and acknowledges it, that new social sciences will develop in the great nineteenth-century like the natural sciences. (He wanted to dedicate *Das Kapital* to Darwin, but Darwin, with enough trouble on his hands already, put him off, saying that he knew nothing about economics.) He took from Saint-Simon, as well as from Hegel, the belief that there are necessary stages of history which circumscribe social action. From this 'scientific' position he mocked as ignorant, blood-thirsty and opportunistic the 'putschism' of Blanqui and his kind (the Militant faction of the day). In the famous last issue of the *Neue Rheinische Zeitung*, printed in defiant red, Marx warned the workers of Cologne against armed revolt. It would be hopeless. The time was not yet ripe. But in 1848 he thought that this revolutionary ripeness of time was only a few years off, not decades or generations. He continued to believe this all his life.[1]

So the *first pillar* of the system was the class struggle as a law of history. He did not so much reject the early socialist belief in natural sociability as argue that under capitalism its only relevant form is the class consciousness of an aroused industrial proletariat. Until that class consciousness emerges, there can be no revolution: when there is, it will come[2]. People are bound by their class situation. Only in a post-revolutionary classless society will all men and women be free and the division of labour become something flexible, voluntary, not imposed. His humanistic vision of an ideal, unalienated life-and-work was not dissimilar to that of Fourier; but it would not come by turning one's back on society in rural retreats, it could only

---

[1]Forty years ago, when a student, I first saw a Communist Party poster advertising a meeting on 'The Coming Collapse of Capitalism'. Few years have passed without a similar sighting, but now only from real crazy break-away, splinter Trotskyite or Militant groups.

[2]Years later Orwell summed up this aspect of Marxism as: 'until there is consciousness there can be no revolution, until there is a revolution there can be no consciousness.'

come through class struggle and almost certainly revolution on the streets.

The bourgeoisie enjoy freedom, and it is real freedom; but they gain it literally at the expense of others and maintain it by controlling a servile class. Yet in their time the bourgeoisie are a progressive and emancipatory force, up to a point. He uses 'bourgeois' as a pejorative adjective in matters of property relations generally, including the subjugation of women — the bourgeoisie treat women as if they are bits of private property. Indeed. He does not use it, however, to condemn the whole of literature and art as being only an instrument of class domination. Such extravagances of Marxist fundamentalists are not canonical.

Bourgeois literature certainly reflects class values. But if we are conscious of that, can see through this conceptual veil, we can discount it and find other things of value. Similarly Marx took for granted traditional republican ideas of citizenship. They were abused, misused and deliberately limited in the class interests of the bourgeoisie; but they were not inherently bourgeois. That became part of Leninist polemic much later.

The *second pillar* of Marx's Marxism was the law of the accumulation of capital. Under capitalism all classes except a large proletariat and a small bourgeoisie disappear. Put simply in the *Manifesto*, under capitalism the rich get richer and the poor get poorer until the system breaks down. The mobility of capital, compared to the fixity of feudal land, leads not, as the great liberal economists had hoped, to perfect competition and a widespread distribution of private property and wealth, but to concentration, exploitation and monopoly. Quite why the breakdown is inevitable is far from clear. There is a 'vulgar Marxist' explanation, officially sanctioned in socialist states: that what he called immiseration will reach such a point that the poor can stand it no longer and will revolt, and the very concentration of capital concentrates the target — a point that anarchists like Bakunin seized upon. But that is too voluntaristic, moralistic and psychological to the scientific Marx, though it is popular and polemical Marxism.

Marx thought that inevitable contradictions arose in the capitalist system because of a dialectical logic of 'the clash of opposites'. This became known as 'historical materialism'. It is the material factors of production that change the nature of societies; not the mere technology, as Saint-Simon had taught,

but the combination of new technology and class ownership —
'the mode of production'. Under capitalism, this was the
factory based on division of labour owned by an entrepreneur.
So long as the bourgeoisie can expand the factors of production, capitalism thrives; but there comes a point when their
self-interest as a class restricts the expansion of production.
That creates a revolutionary situation. Capitalism is contra-
dicting itself. Yet even this is a simplification. The fundamental cause of the crisis is that the accumulation of surplus
value, the exploitation of labour which alone creates the value
of goods, can no longer be reinvested in the system. If, that is,
it is true that the value of goods is directly related to the labour
put into them. Perhaps it should be, but it plainly is not.

Marx used gallons of ink trying 'to objectify' this point. But
the labour theory of value works better as a moral critique of a
free market theory of wages — that wages ought to reflect the
labour put into a job — than as an explanation of wage levels.
Most Marxists, in fact, understand the 'labour theory of value'
moralistically not scientifically. But Marx was obsessive on
this point, and some modern Marxists too. Marx believed that
he was an objective scientist, not an angry and learned socialist
moralist.

The first volume of *Das Kapital* is not written for the average
proletarian activist, unless he or she knows Latin, Greek,
several modern European languages and has read the English
and Scottish economists as well as Hegel. That it exists is
enough. Marxists know that it contains a proof of the contradictions which will lead, given a timely rush and a push, to the
inevitable collapse of the capitalist system. Once you believe
that collapse is inevitable, then the apparent strength of capitalism can actually be used as evidence that it is about to
collapse. In the Preface, for instance, to the 1882 Russian
edition of the *Communist Manifesto*, Marx and Engels
comment on the growth of both Russia and the USA since
1848:

> ... circumstances react in a revolutionary manner upon America
> itself. Step by step the small and middle land ownership of the
> farmers, the basis of the whole political constitution, is succumbing
> to the competition of giant farms; at the same time a mass industrial
> proletariat and a fabulous concentration of capital funds are devel-
> oping for the first time in the industrial regions.

You have to believe in the prior truth of the theory before this 'fabulous concentration' becomes evidence of impending collapse rather than, simply, of the growth of American capitalism. And while the correlation between a small farming economy and the form of the United States constitution is a sound piece of historical materialism, the same conclusion was reached by nearly every other observer; and the original constitution, moreover, has adapted, with whatever imperfections and injustices, to a radically different society or 'stage of capitalism'.

Too often Marx proceeds by what Jon Elster calls in his profound and patient study *Making Sense of Marx* a 'counterfactual' style of argument: we *know* that American capitalism is going to break down *because* the next stage in society is communism. The actual is deduced from the hypothetical, or rather the hypothesis of stages has become dogma: the future can take no other form. If one examines the validity of Marx's claim that his theory of capital accumulation is scientific (indeed what is meant by such a claim, a matter on which Marx and Engels differ), what emerges very clearly is the intense moralism of Marx's case against capitalism — that quality, in Berlin's words, of being 'an avenging force', a 'revolutionary hymn'.

Elster sees four main thrusts in Marx's understanding of capitalism. First, Marx hated its inhuman aspect, that it separated, alienated, man from any sense of being able to realize his talents and purposes in work. And in simple terms, it underpaid, overworked and exhausted people sytematically. Marx did not invent the concept of alienation. The poet Schiller had panicked about routinization, or was profoundly prophetic, at the mere rumour of a factory in Swabia. But underlying Marx's published writing, and explicit in youthful manuscripts, is a profound cultural critique of capitalism — profound, though, one must say, in its sense of the problem rather than of the solution.

Secondly, Marx held that capitalism is unjust. Many Marxists regard this as bourgeois moralism: did not Marx show that all moral ideas are not merely products of a mode of production but instruments of control used by the ruling class? I don't think he did. But even if he did, he could not contain his moral indignation within the restrictions of his own abstract philosophic categories and scientific pretensions. It is impossible to read him without feeling the anger surging through. His was the most elaborate socialist theory of wages. But all socialisms start from a belief that the determination of wages by market forces alone is unjust. Perhaps it is uneconomic as well, but that is an elaborate second thought.

Thirdly, Marx condemned capitalism as irrational and wasteful: it is prone to cycles of over-production and then under-production. One social system gives way to another when it becomes a restraint on the modes of production. Through oppression human resources are wasted and neglected. The bourgeoisie, who were once economically progressive, are now so exploitative and so threatened by an immiserated proletariat that most of their time and energy is spent on politics rather than in economic production. Marx believed, quite as much as Adam Smith, that an urge to economic expansion is the primary human social drive.

And fourthly, he did not so much condemn the international spread of capitalism, the fact that it was trying to make the world one market, but he pointed to the revolutionary implications of this. 'Workers of the world unite': economic history works to global laws and workers of different countries have more common interest than with their ruling classes. That is the general theory, yet obviously in practice economic and social differences are immense. True, but countries at different stages of development are influenced from elsewhere — he thought from the economically more advanced societies. Obviously not all development would be at the same rate. But the difficulty with this argument is that it simply assumes that there is only a single set of tracks on which world history may move, even if some trains go dangerously fast along them and others dangerously slow. Modern Marxists 'explain' why revolutions have not taken place where and when they ought to have done by talking of the 'uneven development' of capitalism in such and such a country. It is a cold day as I write because it is unevenly hot, or a hot day because a cold front is at radically unequal stages of development. As I have said earlier, it may be easier to offer explanations of why some regimes break down than why some others unobligingly haven't.

The Marxist view of economic conditioning oscillates

between being a dogma, that we call 'economic determinism', and being a truism. How does one read and stress Engels's famous, 'We make our own history, but in the first place under very definite presuppositions and conditions. Among these the economic are finally decisive'? Are the first five words to be stressed, or the last five? If both are given equal weight, then the proposition isn't really saying very much. It all depends what 'finally decisive' means. Is it that at the end of any conflict or dispute about policy, the final outcome will be determined not by human will but by economic forces? Or is it simply that all policies must be economically realistic? And the latter view is hardly distinctively socialist; it is liberal in the *laissez-faire* or economistic sense. Marx himself said: 'the mode of production in material life conditions the general character of the social, political and spiritual processes of life.' '*General* character' and 'conditions' (i.e. not 'causes') are unexceptional. That is simply a socialist (or a liberal) framework: it doesn't of itself tell us much, but it tells us what kind of factors to consider — which is useful. The difficulty is not always with Marx's Marxism, though he could be very dogmatic and deterministic (but then in writing about actual events he was far more eclectic and less inclined to explain every twist of Louis Napoleon's policies, say, by the specific stage of development of the mode of capitalist production); the difficulty is with 'vulgar Marxism', whether Marx's or not.

'Vulgar Marxism' says that there is no need to argue about or define or be confined by 'values', all that matters is a correct analysis of the needs of a particular historical situation. Much credence was given to this by the theory of *ideology*. In his polemic *The German Ideology* Marx began by asserting that great Prussian Professors who held State chairs were not independently minded philosophers, but were in fact, and were bound to be, servants of the State: their ideas were merely ideology. But he ended the polemic by proclaiming a general theory that *all* ideas and values are ideological, that is class determined. That is what he said. Whether he meant it is doubtful. Much of his writing does not deny the objectivity of science or the republican values of free citizenship (again Kant's 'the starry heaven above and the moral law within' — Newton and Rousseau) so much as take them for granted.

But many of his followers came to believe that all science and all morality simply served class interests. Only after the revolution will values and human nature become autonomous, ends in themselves and free-willed. Similarly with 'the State'. In theory it was merely 'the executive committee of the bourgeoisie', but in practice the state machine, Marx saw, could take on a life of its own. Yet his followers had no doubts that the state in the hands of workers would inevitably serve the interests of the working class.

What Marx was fundamentally trying to do, entering an existing socialist movement and polemicizing for most of his life against fellow socialists, was to show that there could be no compromise between communism and capitalism; and that a working class movement would inherit state power and urban industry, could not hope to avoid them, either before or after the revolution. History would see to all that. The only compromises to be made were tactical and short-term, to help the growth of a working class movement, possibly party, at a time when the working class had not become fully conscious of its own nature and historical destiny. But it simply has not happened that way.

It was once said of the Victorian positivist philosopher, Herbert Spencer, that his only idea of tragedy was a theory killed by a fact. To some extent classical Marxism has suffered that fate. Capitalism does not work justly but it stubbornly refuses to collapse. Karl Popper wrote of Marx in his *The Open Society and Its Enemies*: 'He was a prophet of a course of history which did not come true; but ... it is much more important that he misled scores of intelligent people into believing that historical prophecy is a scientific way of approaching social problems.' Great reforms in mixed economies — what Marx derided, looking at the British trade unions, as 'Labourism' — have been achieved, and now socialist states look for ways of reintroducing market price mechanisms, that is, some economic freedom without general political freedom — or just enough to allow entrepreneurial spirit but not enough to threaten one party rule. Where Communist regimes have come to power it has not been because of, in any at all obvious sense, 'the collapse of the capitalist system', but by the military defeat of autocracies, the withdrawal of colonial powers and armed insurrection in such circumstances — an ironical vindication of Blanqui (given will and luck) rather than Marx.

The revolution occurred, after all, in the most economically underdeveloped of the European states. It occurred because the Czarist regime was inefficient in its conduct of the war and totally discredited by the suffering of the war and the national defeat. The Bolsheviks had strong theoretical convictions, great courage, audacity, ruthlessness and tactical skill, a sublime sense of history being on their side. But something else is needed to explain fully their coming to power against the odds in Russia — what Machiavelli, the realist, recognized better than the scientific-minded Victorians to be a perennial factor in the human condition: astounding good fortune. But it turned out to be not entirely good fortune for other socialists, nor for millions of people in the new Soviet Union and then in its 'allies'. Because for ever afterwards it became hard for ordinary people to disassociate 'socialism' from what was done by the Communist Party of the Soviet Union. And where hope lingered on unreasonably long that the Russian revolution had not betrayed liberty, equality and fraternity, the judgement of other socialists was impugned, and such 'fellow travellers' were easily branded as either hypocrites or dangerously naive.

Practice

The Russian Revolution was an event that shook the world. But, unlike the French Revolution, in which all friends of reform everywhere could find some stage of it with which to identify, its policies, methods and leadership divided socialists elsewhere from the very start. This is a matter of historical fact which is difficult to recover because of decades of propaganda from Communist Parties that whosoever shall criticize the 'Motherland of Socialism' is objectively 'a capitalist', a 'reactionary' and, as abuse became ever more broad and bizarre under Stalin in the 1930s, a 'fascist' — or delicately put, 'a crypto-fascist'. And, of course, it suits conservatives to picture democratic socialists as simply nervous or covert Bolsheviks. As I write, a British Prime Minister is, almost incredibly, flogging that dead horse again; but she is a shrewd, if somewhat manipulative, judge of public opinion.

Such unfraternal and extravagant Leninist polemic had its roots in Marx's own violent hostility to criticism but also in the precarious position in which the Bolsheviks found themselves following their seizure of power in October 1917, after the far more popular and spontaneous February revolution. They were threatened by all the Great Powers, were the smallest by far of three socialist parties or movements in Russia, and civil war and famine raged as White armies, more divided among themselves than even the socialist parties, attempted a counter-revolution. In such desperate circumstances there were many who were prepared to accept one party rule and terror ('revolutionary justice' was the term) for the duration of the emergency and Lenin's 'dictatorship of the proletariat for the period of transition', as he put it, from socialism to communism. For a while the hopeful everywhere, not simply the credulous, could believe that his slogan 'all power to the Soviets' (the workers' councils that had sprung up by themselves in nearly every city or defeated army unit) actually described what was happening, rather than the rapid increase in the powers of the state and an acceleration of an already excessively centralising administration.

The Russian Communists had divided the international socialist movement even before the revolution. Rosa Luxemburg had warned Lenin as early as 1905 in a congress of exiles that freedom must be the means, not just the final end, of the party's strategy. And she repeated the warning as a denunciation in 1918, only a year before she was murdered in the counter-revolution in Berlin. For Lenin and many of the old Bolsheviks had proved themselves, even in the politics of exile, dogmatic, autocratic and intolerant. They had denounced as a betrayal of socialism, not simply a debatable mistake or a response to different conditions, the 'revisionism' of the largest legal socialist and Marxist party in the world, the German Social Democratic Party. That party stressed evolution rather than revolution, had doubts that *everything* was class determined, and espoused a policy of building up 'a state within a state' by parliamentary means.

Fundamentally Lenin had rejected politics as a practical, natural, compromising and humane activity for the belief that history had created a single true ideology, immediately accessible only to the heightened consciousness of the vanguard of the working class and their leaders, and that it was in the future interests of the whole working class that this must be instituted by whatever means were needed. Human history was a history of violent class oppression, so that violence which hastened on the coming of a classless society and the famous 'withering away of the state' was not only justifiable, in terms of an eventual lessening of human suffering, but was an 'historical necessity'. The present always had to be sacrificed for the future, and they were so sure of the future. But the actual history of the Russian Revolution and the Soviet State disproves any notion of predictable historical necessity.

The great Leninist innovation, hardly present in Marx, was the concept and reality of party rather than movement. The party became convinced that it was the embodiment of the working class, indeed of an international working class, just as clearly as the Jacobin Club had, for a moment of time, believed that it embodied the will of the people, and that anyone who opposed them was opposing the purest expression of that will; even worse, anyone who did not actively support them, or even failed to work hard, was a traitor or a saboteur.

Lenin's doctrine of the dictatorship of the proletariat is well known, as is his argument in *The State and Revolution* and elsewhere that *the* Party was in the vanguard of history. He was an intellectual and marginally more tolerant than Stalin who succeeded him. But the old Leftist view in the 1960s, 'Lenin good, Stalin bad', now seems thoroughly suspect if one simply reads what he wrote and recalls what he did.[3] He would probably have imprisoned or exiled most socialist opposition but killed many fewer people than Stalin; yet his beliefs in absolute historical necessity created the appalling state of mind in which party dissidents were not simply punished but had to be brought, by whatever means, sometimes psychological as much as physical, to confess errors, not to admit to differences. There were no honest differences, only

---

[3]See especially A.J. Polan, *Lenin and the End of Politics* (Methuen, 1984).

unpurged bourgeois deviations.⁴ Their opponents were not even allowed to die honourably, as revolutionaries themselves had often done in autocratic regimes.

Lenin had said that the party embodied the consciousness of the working class, Stalin crudified this into his notorious 'Aside from the influence of the party there is no conscious activity of the workers'. (There can be no Christians without the Church.) Myth has it that Trotsky, hating Stalin and hunted by Stalin, was Lenin's true heir if the famous 'Testament' of Lenin had ever been published. But consider his words, in the Soviet Party Congress of 1924:

> The party in the last analysis is always right, because the party is the single historic instrument given to the proletariat for the solution of its fundamental problems. I have already said that in front of one's own party nothing could be easier than to acknowledge a mistake, nothing easier than to say: all my criticisms, my statements, my warnings, my protests — the whole thing was a mere mistake. I, however, comrades, cannot say that, because I cannot think it. I know that one cannot be right *against* the party. One can be right only with the party, for history has created no other road for the realization of what is right. The English have a saying: 'Right or wrong, my country.' With far greater historic justification we may say: right or wrong, on separate particular issues, it is my party.
>
> [Isaac Deutscher, *Stalin: a political biography*]

It would have made little difference had Trotsky, not Stalin, succeeded Lenin. The three were as one on this point.

Years later Pasternak reflected in his *Dr Zhivago*: 'In all this time something definite should have been achieved. But it all turns out that those who inspired the revolution ... aren't happy with anything that's on less than a world scale. For them transitional periods, worlds in the making, are an end in themselves ... Man is born to live not to prepare for life.'

The words of contemporaries speak better than pages of summary and analysis. Consider these three texts. The first is from Victor Serge in his *Memoirs of a Revolutionary*:

---

⁴Arthur Koestler's novel *Darkness at Noon* is still the best account of this, the interrogation of the old Bolshevik ideologist by the new Stalinist *apparatnik*.

I immediately discerned within the Russian Revolution the seeds of such serious evils as intolerance and the drive towards the persecution of dissent. These evils originated in an absolute sense of the possession of truth grafted upon doctrinal rigidity. What followed was contempt for the man who was different, for his arguments and his way of life. Undoubtedly, one of the greatest problems each of us has to solve in the realm of practice is that of accepting the necessity to maintain, in the midst of the intransigence that comes from steadfast beliefs, a critical spirit towards these same beliefs and a respect for the belief that differs. In the struggle, it is the problem of combining the greatest practical efficiency with respect for the man in the enemy; in a word, of war without hate.

That last statement, republican yet humanistic, is the clearest distinction between the two socialist traditions I know.

Consider the consequences of all this for thought. If liberty and criticism are suppressed or sacrificed for the sake of the revolution or socialism itself, then distinctions we need to make cannot be made. Oppressive commands must not merely be suffered and obeyed but must be applauded and internalized as if the general will is always my individual will. If everything is class ideology then 'the ideologically correct' is determined not by Rousseau's imagined benificent 'Legislator', but by an actual political party — Lenin and Stalin's one. On their logic not merely is there no liberty to criticize the party of the people, but liberty itself becomes everything the party decides to do, and nothing else. Here, our second text, is a poignant and astonishing example.

In 1936 a Russian music critic called Olesha was commanded to recant publically at a writers' congress his liking for the music of Shostakovitch:

The article in *Pravda* deals with a question of principle. It is the opinion of the Communist Party; either I am wrong or the Party is wrong. The line of least resistance would have been to say to oneself, 'I am not wrong' and mentally reject *Pravda's* opinion. In other words by keeping to the conviction that in the case in question the Party had not spoken correctly, I would have granted the possibility that the Party was wrong.

What would have been the result? There would have been serious psychological consequences. The whole framework of our social life is very closely knit together, comrades. In the life and activity of our state nothing moves or develops independently. . . .

If I do not agree with the Party in a single point, the whole picture of life must be dimmed for me, because all parts, all details of the picture are bound together and arise out of each other, therefore there must not be a single false line anywhere.

That is why I agree and say in this matter, in the matter of art, the Party is always right. And it is from this point of view that I begin to think of Shostakovitch's music. I continue to enjoy it. But I begin to recollect that in certain places it always seemed to me somewhat, it is difficult to get the right word, contemptuous.

[International Literature, No. 6, June 1936, p. 88]

'Not a single false line anywhere . . .'! He must have been very frightened but also a very clever time-server or creep. He was clever not to claim an implausibly sudden conversion to Stalin's conservative and ignorant views on modern music; and equally clever to grasp so well and state so slavishly the full logic of the vulgar-Marxist theory of ideology. He exhibits the bottom of the slippery slope on which any one of us can find ourselves once we get into the habit of telling lies for the good of the cause, or more generally accepting that free actions and judgements must always be an 'ideologically' correct calculation of class (more often party) interest. And consider the rigid and almost totally internalized mentality of a regime which actually thinks that other people will be impressed by their publishing such a glib confession in a foreign language magazine.

Our third text shows that with intolerance and without liberty truth suffers or must go into hiding. Socialists should have been the last people to repeat the mistake of pre-industrial autocrats in seeking, grandly, to freeze knowledge and to hold it constant and, pettily, to excuse themselves from simple moral rules like telling the truth. What is 'ideologically correct', comrade, not merely has to be enforced but can then destroy the sense of reality of the leadership itself. That was Orwell's profound argument in his satires *Animal Farm* and *Nineteen Eighty-Four*. The Communist ideologist ends up by believing his own lies — which does not make it easy to deal even with the outside world. A somewhat similar egalitarian and libertarian to Orwell, Ignazio Silone, attended the Comintern in the 1920s as a delegate of the Italian Communist Party. He provided a concrete example of what had gone wrong quite as extraordinary as poor Comrade Olesha adjusting his views on Shostakovitch to those of Stalin's.

They were discussing one day, in a special commission of the Executive, the ultimatum issued by the [British TUC] ordering its local branches not to support the Communist-led minority movement on pain of expulsion. After the representative of the British Communist Party had explained the serious disadvantage of both solutions, because one meant the liquidation of the minority movement and the other the exit of the minority from the trade union, the Russian delegate Piatnisky put forward a suggestion which seemed to him as obvious as Columbus' egg: 'The branches,' he said, 'should declare that they submit to the discipline demanded, and then, in practice, should do exactly the contrary.' The English Communist interrupted: 'But that would be a lie.' Loud laughter greeted this ingenuous objection, frank, cordial, interminable laughter, the like of which the gloomy offices of the Communist International had perhaps never heard before. The joke quickly spread all over Moscow, for the Englishman's entertaining and incredible reply was telephoned at once to Stalin and to the most important offices of State, provoking new waves of mirth everywhere. The general hilarity gave the English Communist's timid, ingenuous objection its true meaning. And that is why, in my memory, the storm of laughter aroused by that short, almost childishly simple little expression — 'But that would be a lie' — outweighs all the long, heavy oppressive speeches I heard during the sittings of the Communist International, and became a kind of symbol for me.

[R.H. Crossman ed., *The God That Failed* 1950, p. 109].

This incident was frightening because laughter is usually on the side of liberty, is a form of liberty, is so often satire aimed at autocrats — sometimes the only form of opposition possible. But this was not the laughter of moral satire, the healthy laughter of free men, this was the laughter of total cynicism, a mocking laughter which sees nothing in the world but naked power. 'They that live by the sword shall perish by the sword.' Any socialism that destroys the liberties of others and destroys truth destroys itself.

Years later, when he had left the Communist Party, Silone wrote in his *The New Machiavelli*:

I cannot conceive of Socialism tied to any particular theory, only to a faith. The more socialist theories claim to be 'scientific' the more transitory they are. But socialist values are permanent. The distinction between theories and values is still not clearly enough understood by those who ponder these problems, but it is fundamental. A school or a system of propaganda may be founded in a collection of theories. But only a system of values can construct a culture, a civilisation, a new way of living together as men.

[Quoted by Michael Foot in *Debts of Honour*].

An Intermezzo of Texts on British Socialism

Let me not summarize the old ground again, but simply offer — as a kind of long footnote to Silone's point — a small anthology of texts to show a contrasting tradition of 'British socialism' and its variety. It is not, indeed, a theoretically self-conscious or theoretically heavily structured tradition. Small wonder Marxist theorists, even British Marxist theorists of the 1960s and 1970s, all but completely ignored it. But it reflects badly on their methods that they did. For three reasons: (i) they ignored something that is much closer to popular thought than Marx and Engels's mighty abstractions — and isn't socialism supposed to arise from popular thought? (ii) what they found inchoate was precisely what classical Marxism has always lacked, an explicit concern with values and ethical considerations; and (iii) it has taken many Marxists far too long to come to terms with nationalism. We are conditioned by both our class and our national position; classical Marxism almost entirely ignored the specificity of national cultures — though some Western Marxists following Gramsci now examine both the political context of culture and the cultural context of politics. But oddly many British socialists seemed to think that culture was valuable in itself. Certainly the combination of ethical theory and evolutionary theory is something distinctive about 'British socialism'.

These are worth reading on their own account and they may trigger other thoughts than mine in the last chapter of this book — which attempt to summarize this tradition and to show that it has as much right to be called socialist, possibly more right, than the one party states called socialist elsewhere.

William Morris
No one who is willing to work should ever fear want of such employment as would earn for him all due necessaries of mind and body.

All due necessaries — what are the due necessaries for a good citizen?

First, *honourable and fitting work*: which would involve giving him a chance of gaining capacity for his work by due education; also, as the work must be worth doing and pleasant to do, it will be found necessary to this end that his position be so assured to him that he cannot be compelled to do useless work, or work in which he cannot take pleasure.

The second necessity is *decency of surroundings*: including (*a*) good lodging; (*b*) ample space; (*c*) general order and beauty. That is (*a*) our houses must be well built, clean and healthy; (*b*) there must be abundant garden space in our towns, and our towns must not eat up the fields and natural features of the country ... (*c*) order and beauty means, that not only our houses must be stoutly and properly built, but also that they be ornamented duly: that the fields be not only left for cultivation, but also that they be not spoilt by it any more than a garden is spoilt: no one for instance to be allowed to cut down, for mere profit, trees whose loss would spoil a landscape: neither on any pretext should people be allowed to darken the daylight with smoke, to befoul rivers, or to degrade any spot of earth with squalid litter and brutal wasteful disorder.

The third necessity is *leisure*. You will understand that in using that word I imply first that all men must work for some portion of the day, and secondly that they have a positive right to claim a respite from that work: the leisure they have a right to claim, must be ample enough to allow them full rest of mind and body: a man must have time for serious individual thought, for imagination — for dreaming even — or the race of men will inevitably worsen.

[Lecture of 23 January, 1884]

Edward Carpenter
At the bottom, and behind all the elaborations of economic science, theories of social progress, the changing forms of

production, and class warfare, lies today the fact that the old
ideals of society have become corrupt, and that this corruption
has resulted in dishonesty of life. It is this dishonesty of personal life which is becoming the occasion of a new class-war,
from whose fierce parturition-struggle will arise a new
ideal — destined to sway human society for many a thousand
years, and to give shape to the forms of its industrial, scientific, and artistic life . . .

The canker of effete gentility has eaten into the heart of this
nation. Its noble men and women are turned into toy ladies
and gentlemen. . . . As for you, working-men and working-
women — in whom now, if anywhere, the hope of England
lies — I appeal to you at any rate to cease from this ideal, I
appeal to you to cease your part in this gentility business — to
cease respecting people because they wear fine clothes and
ornaments, and because they live in grand houses. You know
you do these things, or pretend to do them, and to do either is
foolish . . . It is time for *you* to assert the dignity of human
labour . . .

Be arrogant rather than humble, rash rather than stupidly
contented; but, best of all, be firm, helpful towards each
other, forgetful of differences, scrupulously honest in your-
selves, and charitable even to your enemies, but determined
that *nothing* shall move you from the purpose you have set
before you — the righteous distribution in society of the fruits
of your own and other men's labour, the return to Honesty as
the sole possible basis of national life and national safety, and
the redemption of England from the curse which rests upon
her.

[From *England's Ideal*, 1887]

Sidney Webb

No student of society . . . can doubt that any important
organic changes will necessarily be (1) Democratic, and thus
acceptable to a majority of the people and prepared for in the
minds of all; (2) gradual, and thus causing no dislocation,
however rapid may be the rate of progress; (3) not regarded as
immoral by the mass of people, and thus not subjectively
demoralising to them; and in this country, at any rate;
(4) constitutional and peaceful.

If Socialism is thus neither a Utopia nor a specially violent method of revolution, what, it may be asked, are its distinctive features? It is not easy to reply in a single sentence. The ideas denoted by Socialism represent the outcome of a gradual change of thought in economics, ethics and politics. The Socialist is distinguished from the Individualist, not so much by any special Shibboleth as by a complete difference as to the main principles of social organization. The essential contribution of the century to sociology has been the supersession of the Individual by the Community as the starting point of social investigations. Socialism is the product of this development, arising with it from the contemporary industrial evolution. On the economic side, Socialism implies the collective administration of rent and interest, leaving to the individual only the wages of his labour, of hand or brain. On the political side, it involves the collective control over, and ultimate administration of, all the main instruments of wealth production. On the ethical side, it expresses the real recognition of fraternity, the universal obligation of personal service, and the subordination of individual ends to the common good.

[From *Socialism in England*, 1890]

Beatrice and Sidney Webb
The very discovery of improved industrial methods, by leading to specialisation, makes manual laborer and brain-worker alike dependent on the rest of the community for the means of subsistence, and subordinates them, even in their own crafts, to the action of others. In the world of civilisation and progress, no man can be his own master. But the very fact that, in modern society, the individual thus necessarily loses control over his own life, makes him desire to regain collectively what has become individually impossible. Hence the irresistible tendency to popular government, in spite of all its difficulties and dangers.

[From *Industrial Democracy*, 1902]

Robert Blatchford
One of the favourite arguments of the Gradgrinds in support of competition is the theory of the Survival of the Fittest.

They say that those who fail, fail because they are not fitted to succeed. They say that those who succeed, succeed because they are 'fit'. They say it is the law of Nature that the weakest shall go to the wall, and to the wall with them — and no quarter.

The slumites live in the slums because they are unfit to live anywhere else. The Duke of Marlborough lived in a palace because the intellectual and moral superiority of such a man naturally forced him into a palace.

[From *Merrie England*, 1908]

Ramsey MacDonald

Socialism cannot succeed whilst it is a mere creed; it must be made a movement. And it cannot become a movement until two things happen. It must be the organising power behind a confluence of forces each of which is converging upon it, but not all of which actually profess it as a consciously held belief; it must also gain the confidence of the mass of the working classes. The Social Democratic Federation neglected both of these tasks, the Independent Labour Party busied itself with both of them; the Social Democratic Federation drifted into a backwater, the Independent Labour Party kept in midstream. A study of the fates which overtook each of these bodies is one of the most fruitfully suggestive which offers itself to the student of politics. . . .

The Labour Party is not Socialist. It is a union of Socialist and trade-union bodies for immediate political work — the Social Democratic Party having joined in at first but after a year's co-operation having returned to its isolation in 1901. But it is the only political form which evolutionary Socialism can take in a country with the political traditions and methods of Great Britain. Under British conditions, a Socialist Party is the last, not the first, form of the Socialist movement in politics.

[From the *Socialist Movement* (Home University Library, 1911)].

George Bernard Shaw

Until the community is organized in such a way that the fear of bodily want is forgotten as completely as the fear of wolves already is in civilized capitals, we shall never have a decent

social life. Indeed the whole attraction of our present arrange-
ment lies in the fact that it does relieve a handful of us from this
fear; but as the relief is affected stupidly and parasitic on the
rest, they are smitten with the degeneracy which seems to be the
inevitable biological penalty of complete parasitism. They
corrupt culture and statecraft instead of contributing to them,
their excessive leisure being as mischievous as the excessive toil
of the laborers. Anyhow, the moral is clear. The two main problems of organized society: how to produce subsistence enough
for all its members, and how to prevent the theft of that subsistence by idlers, should be carefully dissociated; for the trium-
phant solution of the first by our inventors and chemists has
been offset by the disastrous failure of our rulers to solve the
other. Optimism on this point is only wilful blindness.

[From Preface to *Androcles and the Lion*, 1911]

Beatrice Webb
One wonders when a generation of leaders of the people will
arise who will have learnt that love and pity for the down-
trodden cannot achieve its end unless the emotion is accom-
panied with honesty of reasoning, careful observation and
accurate statement of facts. Religious ends and scientific
methods are indivisible if mankind is to rise above the brute's
battle for life. . . .

[*Diary*, 17 September, 1920].

Harold Laski
I mean by liberty the absence of restraint upon those social
conditions which, in modern civilisation, are the necessary
guarantees of individual happiness. . . . My thesis involves the
view that if in any state there is a body of men who possess
unlimited political power, those over whom they rule can
never be free . . . Uncontrolled power is invariably poisonous
to those who possess it. They are always tempted to impose
their canon of good upon others, and, in the end, they assume
that the good of the community depends on the continuance
of their power. Liberty always demands a limitation of political authority . . . That is why Pericles insisted that the secret of
liberty is courage.

[From *Liberty in the Modern State*, 1930].

R.H. Tawney

Liberty is composed of liberties. . . . There is no such thing as freedom in the abstract, divorced from the realities of a particular time and place. Whatever else the conception may imply, it involves the power of choice between alternatives, a choice which is real, not merely nominal, between alternatives which exist in fact, not only on paper. . . . It means the ability to do or to refrain from doing, definite things, at a definite moment, in definite circumstances, or it means nothing at all. . . .

A society is free in so far, and only in so far, as within the limits set by nature, knowledge and resources, its institutions and policies are such as to enable all its members to grow to their full stature, to do their duty as they see it, and — since liberty should not be too austere — to have their fling when they feel like it. . . .

To desire equality is not . . . to cherish the romantic illusion that men are equal in character and intelligence. It is to hold that, while their natural endowments differ profoundly, it is the mark of a civilised society to aim at eliminating such inequalities as have their source, not in individual differences, but in its own organisation; and that individual differences, which are a source of social energy, are more likely to ripen and find expression if social inequalities are, as far as practical, diminished.

Socialism . . . must be adapted to the psychology, not of men in general, nor of workers in general, but of the workers of a particular country at a particular period. It must wear a local garb. It must be related, not only to the practical needs, but to the mental and moral traditions of plain men and women, as history has fixed them. It must emphasise primarily what it has in common with their outlook, not the points at which it differs from them. It must not dogmatise or browbeat, but argue and persuade.

[From *Equality*, 1935].

George Orwell

More than anyone else, perhaps, the miner can stand as the type of the manual worker, not only because his work is so exaggeratedly awful, but also because it is so vitally necessary and yet so remote from our experience, so invisible, as it were, that we are capable of forgetting it as we forget the blood in our veins. In a way it is even humiliating to watch coal-miners working. It raises in you a momentary doubt about your own status as an 'intellectual' and a superior person generally. For it is brought home to you, at least while you are watching, that it is only because miners sweat their guts out that superior persons can remain superior. You and I and the editor of the *Times Lit. Supp.*, and the Nancy poets and the Archbishop of Canterbury and Comrade X, author of *Marxism for Infants* — all of us *really* owe the comparative decency of our lives to poor drudges underground, blackened to the eyes, with their throats full of coal dust, driving their shovels forward with arms and belly muscles of steel.

[From *The Road to Wigan Pier*, 1936].

G.D.H. Cole

Individualism and *laissez-faire* quite change their practical meaning when the individual comes to mean in practice a great capitalist trust or a newspaper syndicate with unlimited capital at its back. It is useless to wish these-giants away, or to sigh for the joys of an age of little things. There can be no peace for the soul of man, and no space for the individual to live his own life, till we have learnt by collective action to subordinate these monsters to our needs.

This is our task today and tomorrow — to subdue these giants to our will without making them at the same time the masters of our spirit. I am not a Communist, but a good Fabian Socialist, precisely because I fear that a Communist Revolution, by sweeping too much away, would enthrone in the minds of the new generation the iron spirit of the mass-producing machine, whereas a milder Socialist Revolution could bring to the control of the machine the liberal spirit that values difference, and reckons suffering at a high rate in the scale of things to be put down.

[From the Fabian Society's *Programme for Victory*, 1941].

George Orwell

Nations do not escape from their past merely by making a revolution. An English Socialist government will transform the nation from top to bottom, but it will still bear all over it the unmistakable marks of our own civilization . . .

It will not be doctrinaire, nor even logical. It will abolish the House of Lords, but quite probably will not abolish the Monarchy. It will leave anachronisms and loose ends everywhere, the judge in his ridiculous horsehair wig and the lion and the unicorn on the soldier's cap-buttons. It will not set up any explicit class dictatorship. It will group itself round the old Labour Party and its mass following will be in the Trade Unions, but it will draw into it most of the middle class and many of the younger sons of the bourgeoisie. Most of its directing brains will come from the new indeterminate class of skilled workers, technical experts, airmen, scientists, architects and journalists, the people who feel at home in the radio and ferro-concrete age. But it will never lose touch with the tradition of compromise and the belief in a law that is above the State. It will shoot traitors, but it will give them a solemn trial beforehand and occasionally it will acquit them. It will crush any open revolt promptly and cruelly, but it will interfere very little with the spoken and written word. Political parties with different names will still exist, revolutionary sects will still be publishing their newspapers and making as little impression as ever. It will disestablish the Church, but will not persecute religion. It will retain a vague reverence for the Christian moral code, and from time to time will refer to England as 'a Christian country' . . . It will show a power of assimilating the past which will shock foreign observers and sometimes make them doubt whether any revolution has happened.

But all the same it will have done the essential thing. It will have nationalized industry, scaled down incomes, set up a classless educational system.

[From *The Lion at the Unicorn*, 1941].

Aneurin Bevan
The philosophy of democratic Socialism is essentially cool in temper. It sees society in its context with nature and is conscious of the limitations imposed by physical conditions. It sees the individual in his context with society and is therefore compassionate and tolerant. Because it knows that all political

action must be a choice between a number of possible alternatives it eschews all absolute prescriptions and final decisions. Consequently it is not able to offer the thrill of the complete abandonment of private judgment, which is the allure of modern Soviet Communism and of Fascism, its running mate. Nor can it escape the burden of social choice so attractively suggested by those who believe in *laissez-faire* principles and in the automatism of the price system. It accepts the obligation to choose among different kinds of social action and in so doing to bear the pains of rejecting what is not practicable or less desirable.

Democratic Socialism is a child of modern society and so of relativist philosophy. It seeks the truth in any given situation, knowing all the time that if this be pushed too far it falls into error. It struggles against the evils that flow from private property, yet realizes that all forms of private property are not necessarily evil. Its chief enemy is vacillation, for it must achieve passion in action in the pursuit of qualified judgments. It must know how to enjoy the struggle, whilst recognizing that progress is not the elimination of struggle but rather a change in its terms.

[From *In Place of Fear*, 1952]

Tony Crosland

Liberty and Gaiety in Private Life; the Need for a
Reaction against the Fabian Tradition
Society's decisions impinge heavily on people's private lives as well as on their social or economic welfare; and they now impinge, in my view, in too restrictive and puritanical a manner. I should like to see action taken both to widen opportunities for enjoyment and relaxation, and to diminish existing restrictions on personal freedom.

The first of these requires, it is true, a change in cultural attitudes rather than government legislation. If this were to come about, much could be done to make Britain a more colourful and civilised country to live in. We need not only higher exports and old-age pensions, but more open-air cafés, brighter and gayer streets at night, later closing-hours for public houses, more local repertory theatres, better and more hospitable hoteliers and restaurateurs, brighter and cleaner

eating-houses, more riverside cafés, more pleasure-gardens
on the Battersea model, more murals and pictures in public
places, better designs for furniture and pottery and women's
clothes, statues in the centre of new housing-estates, better-
designed street-lamps and telephone kiosks, and so on *ad
infinitum*. The enemy in all this will often be in unexpected
guise; it is not only dark Satanic things and people that now
bar the road to the new Jerusalem, but also, if not mainly,
hygienic, respectable, virtuous things and people, lacking only
in grace and gaiety.

[From *The Future of Socialism*, 1956].

From the Labour Party Programme 1982

We believe that the creation of wealth is a *social*
process — one which involves the co-operative efforts of
countless men and women. No one person — nor indeed any
one family or group of shareholders — can be said to 'create'
great wealth, great companies or great estates. It is the people
who create; it is the fortunate few, blessed by the customs and
laws of the land, who are deemed to own. *We intend to change
those customs and laws — to begin to load the scales in favour
of greater equality*.

Neil Kinnock

Democratic socialism in the UK belongs to that broad coalition at the heart of British politics which is committed to the
survival and extension of an effective, humane and democratic
society. British socialism, however, has never adopted or
pursued the rigid, codified, or disciplined theories characteristic of European continental socialism. We have had no
shortage of theorists. But ... they represent the variety and
diversity of thought and experience coming from humanists
and Christians, historians, philosophers, sociologists, writers,
practising politicians, co-operators and trade unionists.

British democratic socialism is a tapestry and the thread that
runs through the weave is above all a deep concern with fellowship and fraternity; with *community* and participation.
The emphasis, exemplified in the work of that democratic
socialist *par excellence* (as Gaitskell described
him) — Tawney — is that political economy is not ultimately

a question of economic organisation or historical inevitability, but of *moral* choice and that all social institutions must be subject to a test of moral purpose.

It is that inheritance which has inspired the labour movement since its inception. These are the values which underlie the creation of the National Health Service, the building of public sector housing, the inaugural acts of de-colonisation, the development of comprehensive education, the equal opportunities legislation and a host of other measures where Labour government at national and local level has worked to reduce disadvantage for the primary purpose of enhancing individual liberty and giving people greater control over their own destiny.

That is the objective past, present and future of democratic socialism — individual freedom.

[Fabian Autumn Lecture, 12 November, 1985].

6

6
The Values of
Democratic Socialism

Professor Hayek is probably right in saying that in this country the intellectuals are probably more totalitarian-minded than the common people. But
he does not see, or will not admit, that a return to 'free' competition means
for the great mass of people a tyranny probably worse, because more irresponsible, than the state. The trouble with competitions is that somebody
wins them. Professor Hayek denies that free capitalism necessarily leads to
monopoly, but in practice that is where it has led, and since the vast number
of people would rather have state regimentation than slumps and
unemployment, the drift towards collectivism is bound to continue ...
Such is our present predicament. Capitalism leads to dole queues, the
scramble for markets, and war. Collectivism leads to concentration camps,
leader worship and war. There is no way out of this unless a planned
economy can somehow be combined with freedom of the intellect ...
[Orwell, 1944 reviewing F.A. Hayek's *The Road to Selfdom*]

As we have seen, there are many varieties of socialism. And,
indeed, every new nation claims a unique national form. Many
but not all of these divisions are variations on Marx's themes,
some of which would be quite unrecognizable by and uncon-
genial to their founder.

However, there is also the decentralist, syndicalist and
cooperative tradition of socialism that stems from Proudhon
and Robert Owen. This rejects the economic theory of stages
and holds that capitalism can be destroyed from within by
forming cooperative communities for production. Then there
is the managerial or mixed economy version of socialism
which emerged from both the German revisionists and the
British Fabians: that the capitalist state can be permeated and
controlled for the general welfare. And not to forget what I
technically call 'British socialism' which has its roots in an
eclectic fusion of Robert Owen's cooperative ideas, the
cultural vision of William Morris. Methodist conscience,
Chartist democracy and revisionist Marxism: libertarian,

egalitarian and above all ethical, placing more stress on personal exemplifications of socialist values than on public ownership or class legislation. And also and always there is the anarchist and communitarian criticism of, and example to, these main-stream socialisms.

Is there a common ground core of meaning amid all these revolving and colliding concepts of socialism? I think there is. Put in the simplest and most basic terms, socialism has both an empirical theory and a moral doctrine. The theory is that the rise and fall and the cohesion of societies is best explained not by the experience and perpetuation of elites (which is conservatism), nor by the initiatives and inventions of competitive individuals (which is liberalism), but by the relationship to the ownership and control of the means of production of the primary producers of wealth — in an industrial society, the skilled manual worker. The doctrine asserts the primacy and mutual dependence of the values of 'liberty, equality and fraternity', and it draws on the theory to believe that greater equality will lead to more cooperation than competition, that this will in turn enhance fraternity and hence liberate from inhibition, restriction and exploitation both individual personality and the full productive potential of society.

The theory is not fully comprehensive: in its strictly empirical and characteristically economic form it is dangerously close at times to being purely a doctrine for the skilled industrial worker. When it speaks to and for the poor and the dispossessed, it assumes the kind of grounds for believing in human rights or depicting the quality of a good life that one finds in the Christian tradition and in the writings of Jean-Jacques Rousseau and Immanuel Kant. Attempts to explain the meaning of these doctrines purely in terms of the economic theory seem far-fetched or fatuous. Socialist theory has no more made an entirely original contribution to ethics than it has to aesthetics or to science. While socialist theory and doctrine complement each other in practice, yet neither logically entails the other, nor even together are they fully comprehensive. To think that any political theory or doctrine must be fully, comprehensive is precisely what I have argued elsewhere makes for a totalitarian rather than a political style of thought.

Russian and Chinese Communism have both gone very far in suggesting that there is a correct *socialist* way to do everything — from agricultural research to sexual conduct and artistic production. But this is nonsense, and its meaning is to be found neither in socialist theory or doctrine but rather in the need for uniformity in would-be totalitarian societies. The democratic socialist should cheerfully concede, as did Orwell, that reactionaries can write great poems and novels and socialists poor ones. British socialism has valued culture, but it has never either taken a narrow view of culture as exclusively 'high culture', nor argued that all culture must be class-based and proletarian.

What is more surprising is that there is no distinctively democratic socialist theory of political institutions. What kind of political institutions does socialism need? Most of the answers come in conventional republican or liberal democratic terms, except that working people will or should participate more in what were originally distinctively bourgeois institutions, make more use of these electoral or parliamentary or informative devices. Few liberals would quarrel with this; indeed, this is liberal doctrine except that socialist and liberal theories expect different outcomes from working liberal, representative institutions. The Cooperative movement in Britain, once so important a part of the Labour movement, now seems to have lost its way, certainly lost its old dominance in the High Street consumer market; and while producers' cooperatives as an idea point a way to the future, actual examples in this country have been few in number and provide no real experience to draw upon, certainly not enough to enter into the general consciousness of the Labour movement, still less of the electorate. Only the commune and the soviet have emerged historically, and then so briefly, as distinctively socialist institutions. But few think that the spirit of Marx's somewhat inconsistent if passionate championing of the Paris Commune of 1870 as the very model of a classless society, still haunts the Soviet Union, even though the Czechoslovak revisionists in 1968 in the 'Prague Spring' invoked the memory of the Commune as if someone in Moscow still cared or could be shamed. But certainly even when some socialists talk like tough guys about 'taking over the State', whether by parliamentary or other means, to use it for wholly socialist policies, then almost at once, a somewhat contradictory and equally socialist reaction and argument arises — one which stresses face-to-face institutions, decentralization, regionalism, local communities and industrial democracy as being both the school and the final resting place of socialist values.

Yet socialists do have a distinctive *attitude* to political and social institutions. They are sceptical that institutions of State or those set up by the State in democratic but non-socialist regimes are always as neutral as they claim to be. This is a healthy scepticism, so long as everyone is aware that they are normally dealing with relative, not absolute, degrees of bias, as with well meant but ultimately impossible attempts at pure neutrality. But if socialists expect 'fair play' they are foolish. Yet if they try to change the rules, say of the press or broadcasting, to get 'fair play', they should remember the suspicion the majority of their fellow countrymen still view them with, and will continue to view them with precisely because they aim to change the known world, and precisely because most regimes called socialist in the world are despotic.

Socialist theory when applied to history can demonstrate that great changes are possible, but must also comprehend that everything cannot change at once and that social systems are rarely as systematic as either classical Marxist theories or classical liberal theorists have supposed. Marxist theories of a complete indoctrination or 'socialization' by education or the media can induce either despair or a rage for violent, instant and utter change. But the 'systems' are in fact so full of imperfections and inconsistencies that, as conservatives often complain, many unexpected opportunities are given to the politically literate radical. Even in the industrial world, mixed economies are not simply facades: they are remarkably mixed. The mixture can be worked upon and varied. Differential advance in different sectors is possible, despite the preconceptions of systematic theory.

The ideas of free citizenship and of political activity had their origins in what were, broadly speaking, the aristocratic cultures of Greece and Rome or among the merchant and bourgeois classes of England, France, Holland, Scotland, Sweden and the German and Italian 'free cities'. Even in those societies it was always difficult to prevent any public example of liberties being exercised among the few from exciting the emulation of at least some of the many. Example or mimesis is a basic social mechanism. The source and enduring myth of republican ideas and institutions came from slave-holding cultures of Greece and Rome; but this does not taint the seed. In many ways the classical ideal of free citizenship is not so much superseded by Marx in his critique of capitalist society as assumed by him. If all this was not part of his own cultural preconceptions, it would be hard to make sense of his fragmentary, undeveloped but important accounts of what is this autonomous human personality that can be emancipated from the alienating, competitive conditions of an industrial society where man seems divorced from the fruits of his labour. In his early *Critique of Hegel*, for instance, he wrote that 'the essence of *man* is the *true community* of men' and that 'men, not as abstractions but real, living, particular individuals are this community. As they are, so it is too.' Marx was much closer to both the classical and humanist traditions and to the French Enlightenment than many of his most famous disciples.

Thus it is historically false to identify most of the characteristic political institutions of modern 'liberal democracy' with the rise of the capitalist market. Here the theory is often in error. Capitalism accelerated the spread of such institutions through their instrumental use both to liberate new productive forces and to impose new types of control on the working class. Even so, the political and educational concessions involved in establishing a manipulative facade of free institutions proved more important than either side once thought, ultimately threatening any simple class control of the system. The skilled working man needed by the new factories and the new technologies was a very different human animal from the peasant typical of the agricultural mode of production in autocracies. He had to be literate, for one thing, and was dangerously concentrated in cities, for another, even in capital cities. It was difficult to stop him from organizing trade unions, even in restraint of trade, without denying him the skills that the economy demanded. He was a constant threat to the State precisely because its power and wealth came more and more to depend upon his abilities. Small concessions in the franchise always proved the thin edge of a wedge. And many of the new weapons of control proved double-edged. His new masters had to educate him and, for instance, quite naturally, sought to control that education and to limit it narrowly. But on the scale demanded, teachers were both hastily trained and hard to control completely. They began to constitute a new intelligentsia or at least a special subsection of the middle class, open to new secular ideas and still full of old evangelical ones; and even the oldest ideas of those who taught them were heavily contaminated, through Latin and Greek, with the classical myth of free citizenship. And gradually ideologies of progress began to replace myths of the 'good old days'. When the pupils emerged from the partial dark of such utilitarian school rooms, they often saw rudimentary democratic institutions existing already.

Some leaders of opinion like John Stuart Mill argued that the mass of the people should come into their own and exercise political power, if and when they were fully educated; and that if they were fully educated, they would — which was not what happened. Others sought to postpone that fearful democratic dawn by restricting education. But the very demands of capitalist technology for skilled and literate workers, quite apart from radical and socialist agitation, both heightened the crisis and the demands, if not for new political institutions, at least for accelerated popular access to existing ones.

As well as institutions and theories, values are important. When ordinary people say that they now do not know what the Labour Party stands for, it is unlikely that they are thinking of organization, the details of policy in manifestos or are striving for 'the correct theoretical perspective'. Whether we are followers of Labour Parties, Social Democratic Parties or of 'true socialism' (in one or other of its 57 varieties), values are always involved. Those who 'unmask' the hidden curriculum in education, for instance, can themselves be bitten as they bite, or at least asked politely to come clean whether they believe their holy and objective selves to be 'value free' or simply to hold the right (class) values. Not all hidden values are oppressive; many, like good habits, are benign. There is no objection to people believing that they are right, only to believing that other people must always be wrong. Everything depends on *how* values are held and asserted and on *how* they are related to other values. Even if we have difficulty tolerating the values of others, we should at least notice that our own values are not likely to be always in perfect harmony in every circumstance.

Any values to be realized in the real world keep company
with other values and often contradict them. We cannot,
indeed, have both complete equality and complete liberty, but
I don't want either alone: the one mediates the other. Also
some values are asserted as procedures and some as goals: we
may be sure *what* we want to do, but equally sure that it should
not be done *that* way. 'Liberty', for instance, can be both a
procedural value and a goal. But because no single practice or
policy follows from theory in every circumstance, it is our
values that mainly decide what alternative policies to
follow — what route is *best*.

Two schools of thought, however, seem unwilling to debate
what values we should hold, and often seek to avoid talk of
values at all: determinist Marxism and managerial pragmatism. Marx himself in his early writings, as we have suggested,
seemed to take for granted both the classical tradition of free
republican citizenship and a view of human nature found in
Kant. He also did not believe, like many of his disciples, that
all present values are simply class values and would be wholly
different in a classless society.

Liberty, equality and *fraternity* are the specifically socialist
cluster of values — if one treats 'cooperation' and 'community' as closely related to 'fraternity'. Only equality is specifically socialist in itself: liberty and fraternity, however, take
on a distinctively socialist form when the three are related to
each other. And the three values themselves presume that individuals are both agents and the objects of values, although
individualism, as I will suggest, can take on a specifically
socialist form.

Liberty

Liberty deserves almost fanatic support from democratic
socialists; a truly socialist movement is so committed to more
liberty and to more open government that at times it can seem
almost incoherent among the multitude of small, good causes
which run across the stage of the movement, whether scripted
or not, and find support in the wings. And at times it can seem
almost paranoiac in its belief that anything less than totally
open government is likely to be concealing oppressive weapons

behind every lazily or habitually closed door. Liberty, by itself, is indeed an exuberant and unpredictable thing. The actions of free men are always unpredictable: this is why bureaucrats dislike citizens and why some councillors try hard to stop their tenants painting their houses differently or keeping this or that kind of pet animal. Here is the unavoidable tension between the theory of socialism and its moral beliefs in local practice. And some 'libertarians', who call themselves socialists and who join socialist movements, seem to believe that anything goes so long as it is an authentic action of an untrammeled personality or of a disadvantaged minority group. If I bite, I bite freely and splendidly.

Such political 'street theatre' is a cross that any democratic socialist movement in a free society must bear as cheerfully as it can. But true socialists are concerned with judging morally the social consequences of individual and minority group actions quite as much as with writing accounts of human action in social terms: even here values must be asserted clearly. Bad social conditions do lead to increased delinquency for instance, but this does not justify delinquency — it only affects our theories of how to diminish it and our views on sentencing policy. True socialists examine how even the most 'authentic' individual actions, whether of violent protest or colourful self-assertion, can affect the equal rights of others or diminish rather than enhance fraternity. The Labour Party is proud to have gathered so many vociferous minorities into its ranks; but the liberated must mediate their liberties to those of others, and study how they can be part of the greater whole. It may be liberty, but it is neither right nor politic for a hundred tails to shake one dog. And winning a vote on policy at a Party conference may or may not be relevant to winning a General Election.

Liberty is not, we have argued, to be abandoned as a bourgeois concept or on account of its origins. But it need not remain in the narrow nineteenth century tradition of 'freedom from', simply of not being interfered with by the state or powerful neighbours. Sir Isaiah Berlin has eloquently argued, in his famous essay '*Two Concepts of Liberty*', the danger of thinking of liberty in other than negative terms: if we give any positive content to liberty, ascribe to it any objectives, then we end up, all too often, crying out like Rousseau to 'force people

to be free' — as it were, 'here is your Welfare State, damn you
(or bless you); now you are free!' And the social worker is
King, or Queen. The warning is salutary. Reformers have
need to watch it. In any possible society, socialist societies
included, people may not like what they are given and must be
free to challenge by public debate (or by turning their backs on
it all) both values and policies. But even our good negative
liberties ultimately depend on positive political action. The
positive assertion of liberty is needed to open doors, to create
an open society; but then we do not just sit admiring so many
choices of ways forward or to exit, we need to choose, by free
and open debate, the best doors to go through and then move
on — although perhaps never, indeed, completely shutting
any. People who use their liberty to avoid political life are
more often done down than left in peace. The price of liberty is
even higher than eternal vigilance, as Lincoln sadly said: it
demands eternal action. If people have not been accustomed
or allowed in the past to act as equal citizens, say women in
general, say the black population in particular, or the Catholic
minority in Northern Ireland, then they must not merely have
the prohibitions removed, but the disadvantaged must be
given positive encouragement and positive inducements to use
their liberty. Freedom needs its antique, republican, pre-
liberal cutting edge restored in modern conditions: freedom is
positive action in a specific manner, that of a citizen acting as
if among equals; and not merely to preserve rights and welfare
of existing citizens (says the socialist) but to extend them to the
disadvantaged and the wretched of the earth.

Socialists must add the egalitarian assumption to liberty
that not merely must all men and women be treated as citizens,
but also be helped to count equally as citizens and, above all,
expected to act as citizens. Liberty in this positive sense of
public action does not deny liberty in the more liberal, negative sense of being left alone and in peace: it subsumes,
complements and extends it. A free man or woman must move
back and forth between public and private life, both the richer
for the other. Citizens in socialist societies must have rights
against the State as well as a duty to work for commonly
agreed purposes. This is what stirred the world in the example
of Polish 'Solidarity'. R.H. Tawney long ago argued the com-
plementarity of rights and duties in his great essays *The*

Acquisitive Society and *Equality*. We are foolish to leave all talk of duties to the other side.

Thus talk of socialist liberty as being completely different from bourgeois liberty is melodramatic nonsense. Many left-wingers who are libertarians both at heart and in their personal behaviour get themselves trapped in their writings in a bad piece of Marxist logic: that only in the classless society after the revolution can there be true liberty — until then all we have is capitalist liberty and an 'repressive tolerance' (a phrase of the late Herbert Marcuse). 'Thank God for small mercies', say men actually living in oppressive regimes. Socialists must always try to extend liberty to more and more people and to more and more activities in whatever circumstances possible. They must at least try to persuade those who think that liberty is being left alone in comfort to watch the television or to cultivate one's garden, that governments rarely leave people alone or treat justly those who will not stand up for themselves and combine politically.

Often the most passionate anti-socialist arguments come not from liberals who dogmatically believe that liberty depends on the free working of the market mechanism, but from liberal élitists who think that liberty is all very well for the likes of us but an impossible proposition *en masse* for the likes of them. They fear not so much an egalitarian political tyranny, whatever their rhetoric, as a debasement of their culture. Perhaps they flatter themselves too much to think that it is their culture that popular politicians wish to universalize and hence debase or vulgarize. Their real defence is that their culture is in itself a free activity, irrelevant to political consid-erations except in totalitarian regimes, unless they themselves try to make it so by claiming either that educated elites should rule by virtue of their culture, or should have their special culture specially subsidized by the state. The argument in Britain, for instance, that the existence of private education is the absolute test case of freedom, would be more impressive if the private schools were not so brazen in arguing that their education constitutes a good investment. Property rights and educational rights are, indeed, closely linked in both conserva-tive and liberal doctrine.

'In so far as the opportunity to lead a life worthy of human beings is needlessly confined to a minority', wrote R.H.

Tawney, 'not a few of the conditions applauded as freedom would more properly be denounced as privilege. Action which causes such opportunities to be more widely shared is, therefore, twice blessed. It not only subtracts from inequality, but adds to freedom'.

As liberty is maximized it will become more participative and positive, more distinctively socialist. Yet always free participation will bring many voices not one; refusal to hear criticism can be no more a virtue in socialist societies than in conservative; and no multiplication of opinions, however dramatically contrived, can guarantee 'truth' or sensible decisions about means and ends. If journalists are allowed liberty, they will criticize and sometimes abuse governments and even Labour leaders; and if council tenants are treated as citizens, they may choose tasteless curtains, prefer cash to standard decorative schemes and not always welcome unannounced visits from social workers and council officials with proper enthusiasm. 'Participatory democracy' like 'liberty' is often a very rough and ready, all too human business, as well as a necessary condition of social justice; yet it is far from a sufficient condition. What is it all for?

Equality

Anyone who can honestly call themselves a socialist must agree that equality is the basic value in any imaginable or feasible socialist. society; and further that egalitarian behaviour and example is a necessary part of building any road to socialism. For this reason, presumably, some members of the Labour movement do not ordinarily choose to call themselves 'socialist' at all, not merely from prudential reasons — that the majority of our fellow countrymen are not stirred by the word, or if so somewhat negatively, but because they honestly and, to them, realistically hope only for a more compassionate and concerned welfare society, with a high Beveridge minimum but with a moralized, talented and public-spirited rotating hierarchy (in other words, 'Labourism', 'social democracy', whether in or out of the Labour Party). Governing in such a spirit is not to be despised. It may even be seen as a necessary staging post. It would be a great deal better than our present society; indeed we thought we had it securely but now we have lapsed back thanks to deliberate actions of governments (in practical terms of the greatest happiness of the greatest number, I would rather see a Lab-Lib coalition than a pure Socialist Opposition). But this moderate spirit perpetuates some of the causes of injustice and the unacceptable inequalities that it seeks to ameliorate; and it is an unnecessarily limited ambition.

If we are thoughtful and careful, there is no necessary contradiction between equality and liberty. But difficulties have to be faced. It is quite possible to have societies in which the mass of the population are, in de Tocqueville's words, 'isolated but equal', with only a small and even a benign governing class. Montesquieu had pictured 'oriental despotism' as being of this kind, vast masses of roughly equal peasantry under a small military and administrative elite. This is what some Left-Marxist opponents meant when they accused Stalin and, later, Chairman Mao, of creating a new form of oriental despotism. The hallmark of 'despotism' was, to all these writers, the lack of intermediate social grades typical of both European feudalism and modern autocracy. So equality of condition is not necessarily socialist: it can be despotic. This dark thought has been a common imagined feature in London's *The Iron Heel*, Zamyatin's *We*, Huxley's *Brave New World* and Orwell's *Nineteen Eighty-Four*. I actually prefer to speak of an egalitarian society rather than an equal society. Even so, without a sincere desire to achieve an egalitarian society, any democratic socialist movement loses its dynamic and lapses back into a directionless pragmatism and the paternalism of a benevolent hierarchy: in homely terms, the councillor and the social worker perpetually sad that their people are not grateful for their efforts on their behalf, and cannot be trusted to make collective decisions for themselves without untidy results.

The concept of equality, however, has notorious difficulties and is often parodied: a literal and exact, universal equality, whether of opportunity, treatment or result is almost as undesirable as it is impossible. Equality of opportunity, even if obtainable, could only be a one-off affair, a way of reshuffling or new-dealing the pack — unless everyone was childless and there was no inheritance of property, skills or even predispositions. Equality of result would either be, indeed, the death of liberty or a response to a very precise specification of particular areas, such as income, for instance, but not necessarily all work, trade or barter in leisure time. Nevertheless an egalitarian society is both conceivable and desirable. Certainly some societies are remarkably less unequal than others; but if by an egalitarian society is meant a classless society, one in which everybody would see each other as sister and brother, of equal worth and potential, then one can readily imagine a genuinely fraternal society with no conceit or constraint of class. It would not be a society in which everyone was exactly equal in power, status, wealth and acquired abilities, still less in end-products of happiness; but it would be a society in which none of these marginal differences were unacceptable and regarded as unjust by public opinion — a public opinion which would itself become, as gross inequalities diminished, far more critical and active, far less inert and fatalistic than today. These margins would remain perpetually ambiguous, open, flexible, debatable, a moving horizon that is never quite reached, irreducible to either economic formula or legislative final solution; but less intense and less fraught with drastic consequences than today.

No difficulties about the concept are so great as to warrant abandoning it or treating it purely as the liturgy of the socialist church. One difficulty is that socialists want, rhetorically and politically, to make something sound positive which is philosophically best stated in negative terms. There is no 'complete equality' which can 'finally be realized', unless genetic engineering were to come to the aid of economic planning (with about equal accuracy and predictability, one would hope). But there are so many unjustifiable inequalities. Poverty, for instance, limits life and the exercise of freedom in nearly every possible way, and if riches or affluence give undoubted freedom to their possessors, it is usually at the cost of their humanity and fellow feeling. If we believe in the moral equality or the fraternity of all mankind, then *all* inequalities of power, status and wealth need justifying. The boot should be worn on that foot. Inequalities can be justified only if these inequalities can be shown to be of positive advantage to the less advantaged. Some inequalities can be justified, many not — particularly if one adds the vital condition of democratic citizenship: actually to ask the disadvantaged and to depend on their reply. No precise agreement is ever likely to be reached or, if so, only for a particular time and place. Nor can philosophy supply incontrovertible criteria for what is an unjustifiable inequality. Each case will stand on its merits and opinions will differ. But the important point is to see that inequalities of reward and power are unjustifiable in principle unless some clear public benefit follows from them that could not otherwise exist.

Here I am following the arguments of John Rawls in his monumental *A Theory of Justice* and of W.G. Runciman in his *Relative Deprivation and Social Justice*. Their arguments have been dismissed by some socialists as merely a radical form of liberalism. But even if that was their intent, if in fact all inequalities were called into question, constantly questioned, criticized and forced to justify themselves in the public interest, then one would at least be in a society with a dominant egalitarian spirit. The vast differences in power, status and wealth that are in fact acceptable to most peoplle in a class-conscious society, will grow less tolerable as income differences diminish and as egalitarian spirit grows, by argument, agitation and example, as well as by legislation.

Equality does not mean sameness. Men and women, not robots, animate an egalitarian spirit. The idea that even a strict and absolute equality of condition would destroy human individuality and character is not so much a Tory journalist's nightmare as a science fiction fantasy. Are most of the things we most enjoy doing in life likely to be repetitive and 'the same' if they are always done between two people, walking and talking together, who might have, whoever they were, roughly equal income and the same, or no, social class? The fears of Tory and 'market liberal' authors that high taxation and state intervention will necessarily destroy individuality are literally absurd. Do they really think that man is so artificial and individuality so fragile? Can they really not imagine that everyone could have roughly the same standard of living, equal status and equal access to the processes of political power and yet still retain individuality? Or can they, more understandably, simply not imagine how their fancy selves could adjust to such a society? For some people genuinely believe that individuality, character and culture only exist among the prosperous and well-educated, and that 'the masses', as the Natives used to, 'all look the same'. Masses can be generalized about but not the educated and the gentry! It is the saddest fate of the poor to have even their individuality removed from them in principle as well as threatened in practice. Charles Dickens, H.G. Wells and George Orwell had a different view of the matter: they actually romanticized poverty as a school of eccentricity and character: it was the middle class who were conventional, nervous of their neighbours and socially timid. Intellectually the alliance is a strange one between the elitist snobbery of Cambridge Toryism, the contemporary high priests of the cult of inequality, and the competitive men of the market who claim that high taxation destroys 'initiative'. I suppose a Marxist would say that what they have in common is class interest.

Tawney in 1931 argued (in the passage quoted in Chapter 5) that equality was best seen simply as the negation of socially imposed inequalities, and inequalities actually repress not express natural, individual differences. He argued further that a socialist society would have more diversity in it, not less, when he expressed

> straightforward hatred of a system which stunts personality and corrupts human relations by permitting the use of man by man as an instrument of pecuniary gain. The socialist society envisaged . . . is not a herd of tame, well-nourished animals, with wise keepers in command. It is a community of responsible men and women working without fear in comradeship for common ends, all of whom can grow to their full stature, develop to their utmost limit the varying capacities with which nature has endowed them.

Now 'less unjustifiable inequality today!' and 'no unjustifiable inequality tomorrow!' may not be slogans that 'warm the blood like wine', but that may be fortunate. For 'Forward to Equality' is more likely to warm the hearts of party activists than those whom they need to persuade. In practice in modern societies not only trade unionists are highly interested in differentials. And philosophically no one value, be it liberty, equality, fraternity, love, truth, reason, even life itself (as Thomas Hobbes taught) can at all times override all the others or be sure never to contradict them. Equality could certainly be maximized in a totalitarian state; but only at the expense of liberty, so that genuine fraternity is destroyed. The political socialist, who knows that democracy must be the means as well as part of the end, having a theory of society, looks at values together, both in their social setting and in relation to each other. He no more postpones liberty until the classless society than he reserves egalitarian and fraternal behaviour and example until the classless society. If he does, he will not get there; and when he does, classlessness by itself will not have solved all problems and removed all possibilities of injustice.

The political socialist as egalitarian need not get drawn into the parody argument which assumes exact equality of income and wealth: that is somebody else's nightmare, not his dream. Literal-minded distributive socialism is very hard to find. 'Soak the fat boys, and spread it thin' may be good populist rhetoric, but most people know it would be thin indeed unless new productive forces arise. Industrial relations are bad, not because the workers on the shop floor believe that the cow can be milked without being fed; they are bad because people think that it is unfair or unjust that they should be restrained in their wage demands while their bosses actually write to tell newspapers that people with high incomes have no incentive to work harder unless income tax is cut and their children can freely inherit all their wealth. Workers, oddly, use their eyes and see how much patriotic restraint in expenditure and overseas investment is practised by those who at least try hard to look like ruling classes and British industrialists.

Socialism claims that with greater equality there can be greater fraternity, hence greater co-operation, hence greater productivity since wealth basically comes from the worker. 'Working together' should be the popular slogan of democratic socialism, not the old condescending 'Labour Cares' or the self-deception that the man in the street would be a theoretical socialist but for the mass media. Working together creates the conditions for equality and an atmosphere of fraternity. Power, special skill and status also count for a lot, but so does having a clear and worthwhile job. Real managers like to produce; real leaders carry followers with them, learn from them and take their successors from the ranks; but the English upper middle class now more and more prefer banking to industry and spend much of their income ensuring that their own children succeed them.

So much scope for action (and alternative actions) remains in the business of moving towards a far greater equality; and this is not to be represented as jealous levelling but rather as a constant, aggressive questioning of the reasons for and the justifications of both existing distribution of incomes and wealth and the existing divisions of responsibility between 'workers' and 'management'. Such questioning could prove as popular as it is right. More important for socialism than abstract arguments about formal ownership is progress towards taking all wages and income out of the market and determining them by representative arbitration and open comparison of relativities. Public policy should work towards complete openness of all incomes and towards a minimum and a maximum income. If people's incomes were known, they would have to be justifiable. Many differences can, on examination and after open discussion, be justified. But they need to be. *We need to develop this as a whole new branch of applied social philosophy rather than of traditional economics.*

Socialist theory *began* as a critique of the theory of wages in the classical economics of Adam Smith and Ricardo: simply that they are unjustly determined in market economies. Free trade unions need free collective bargaining, indeed, as a great but minimal achievement in a market economy. The result, however, is not social justice in any sense, still less 'equality' (even of opportunity), precisely because trade unions rarely constitute even a majority of the working population, even before long-term mass unemployment returned to mixed economies. In a socialist and egalitarian economy their collective power will concentrate on reaching agreement about general procedures for arbitrating wage differentials as part of the whole complex of real income, not on a multiplicity of local or industry-wide conflicts with employers. Half-way houses will be many in the evolution of an agalitarian society: wage, welfare and tax structure will all take a long time to come together (many still do not see the need nor perceive the connection); and different institutions will evolve in different societies and even in different parts of the United Kingdom. But the essential step forward must be the establishment of a guaranteed national social wage, set at a level not simply to avoid the pain of poverty, but to create equal opportunities for full citizenship and participation in everything that is held to be part of the good life,[1] and the limiting of top incomes to a level that does not create life styles or opportunities for inheritance that frustrate the objectives of the social wage. Poverty is not just not starving, it is being shut out from all the things that public opinion holds necessary for a decent life. Neither minimum nor maximum can be decided *a priori*; they are a matter for continuing experiment and open debate.

If economic equality is a relative concept, there is one definition of equality that should be absolute: to end the different rates of mortality between social classes or to gain equality of life and death. The matter is flagrant. Even in a still relatively prosperous country such as Great Britain in a reasonably good year, 1971, the death rate for adult men in social class V (unskilled workers) was nearly *twice* that of adult men in social class I (professionals). The 'neo-natal death rates' (deaths in the first month of life) were also *twice* as high, and for the period from one month to one year, actually *five* times higher.[2] Quite simply, this is morally wrong and is avoidable. Well-off conservatives, when confronted with such figures, simply will not believe them, will sneer at 'statistics' or — sometimes quite literally — repress them. In an odd way, it is to their credit as human beings that they choose not to face such facts, rather than to admit them as a justifiable price for inequality.

National comparisons of infant mortality and death rates between poorer and richer countries tell an even more ghastly tale. By a common definition of 'less-developed' societies, the average lifespan of men and women taken together is 42 years, and in developed countries it is 71. Quoting these figures, a philosopher discussing possible justifications of violence says: 'It is not too much to say that what we have before us are different kinds of lifetime.'[3] The 'Brandt Report' on world poverty and 'North-South' relations simply and prudentially

---

[1] See Peter Townsend, *Poverty in the United Kingdom: A Survey of Household Resources and Standards of Living*, Penguin 1979.

[2] See the 'Black Report', *Inequalities in Health: Report of a Research Working Group*, DHSS, London 1980, p. 1, (republished as Peter Townsend & Nick Davidson (eds), *Inequalities in Health*, Penguin 1982).

[3] See Ted Honderich, *Three Essays on Political Violence*, Oxford 1977.

argued that the disparities were so huge that soon the *peace* of
the world will depend on a massive reallocation of resources.

The gaps between the social classes even in a relatively
wealthy country like Britain are great not merely in the precision of death, but in the more general incidence of ill-health.
In his Galton lecture in 1975 Sir John Brotherston (a former
high Civil Servant) said: 'For the most part the evidence suggests that the gaps remain as wide apart as a generation ago
and in some instances the gaps may be wider.'[4] Thomas
Hobbes based his philosophy of political obligation on the
alleged necessity of individuals to surrender all power to a
State that could effectively minimize the chances of violent
death. A modern Hobbes might set his sights higher and see
the power of the State at its highest when it can maximize the
life expectancy of its inhabitants, and at its most precarious
when it fails to do so. Certainly if there was no difference in
the death rate between social classes, we would know that we
no longer had social classes. This is a fairly obvious if unusual
definition of a classless society: one in which life expectancy is
equal. If governments will not move towards such equality,
small wonder that some would tear them down irrespective of
liberty. Life and death are intrusive matters.

The cult of inequality has strangely survived the demise of
aristocratic society. Even Americans are noticeably more
egalitarian than the British. Even the Scots and the Welsh are
noticeably more egalitarian than the English. As Tawney
argued, dead creeds often survive as habits. But of late the
'habits' have been revitalized as ideology: the strange
amalgam in 'Thatcherism' of free market economics and
traditional hierarchical thinking. An egalitarian should feel no
shyness in challenging that. For it is overwhelmingly likely
that there will be more exercise of human freedom, not less, as
unemployment, poverty, and class differences in sickness and
mortality, type and length of education, and of income, are all
diminished.

Again, the democratic socialist as egalitarian is not a
believer in literal equality. One argues on two fronts: against

---

[4]Quoted in the Introduction to the 'Black Report', *op. cit.*

both the 'no holds barred' of neo-conservatism and against
the utopianism of 'nothing less than complete equality of outcome' of what I still regressively call 'student (or is it infan-
tile?) Marxism'. Even if there was equality of incomes, only a
totalitarian regime could even try to ensure literal equality of
outcome: to control completely all *uses* of income and labour
other than consumption, all leisure-time labour, all do-it-
yourself even for sale or barter.[5] But the converse is equally
true. If anyone fears that equality of incomes by itself would
lead to uniformity, they are simply wrong. And if anyone
hopes that economic equality by itself would lead all people to
treat each other as equals, they are very hopeful. It is a necessary but not a sufficient condition for us treating each other as
equals.

In an egalitarian society, that is a society which respects
human equality and dislikes hierarchy, and in a society with
far greater equality of social condition than ours, individual
talents could flourish without those restrictions of poverty or
even relative deprivation which unfairly limit the quality of life
of some and unfairly advantage others. In his *Relative
Deprivation and Social Justice*, W.G. Runciman argued that it
is a moral imperative to *respect* all men and women equally,
but not to *praise* all equally. Yet it does not follow that
disproportionately 'praised' or admired talents or skills
should carry with them directly proportionate rewards. Neo-
conservatives crudely assume that differential talents will not
be exercised unless there is a directly commensurate economic
reward: that high taxation destroys and lower taxation
enhances initiative. This crude reductionism needs to be challenged. Praise can be sought as an end in itself. People's desire
to exercise particular functions — unhappily including power
over others — bears little relation to marginal increases or
decreases of economic reward. There is a deep, human instinct
to enjoy and admire the job well done, and deep satisfaction
too in working together, in togetherness, sociability, mutual
aid. Those who doubt it should try it sometime. If not they
miss some of the best experiences in life.

_____

[5]See Alec Nove, *The Economics of Feasible Socialism*, London 1983.

The democratic socialist's concept of the individuals is more humane and plausible than the Hobbesean-utilitarian assumption of man-the-competitive-atom that underlies both neo-liberal and neo-conservative thought. The socialist sees the individual as achieving his or her identity as a person through sociability. We are all unique individuals, indeed, but we uniquely interact with others; and who we are is shaped as much by other's perceptions of what we do and say as by our effect upon them. This is a subject in itself. But we can say both that a moral belief in equality brings out the individuality of each other person, and that more equal social conditions and more tasks done and decisions made cooperatively, whether in firm, factory, school or voluntary body, would create a cumulatively greater respect for the equality of others.

So an egalitarian spirit arises out of protest as well as reason. But reason must tell us that true equality is no more but no less than the removal of all unjustifiable inequalities: and that it is a necessary condition, but not a sufficient condition for democratic socialism. 'Equality' needs to be related not merely to liberty, but to that most rhetorical, potent, but least defined of values, 'fraternity'. We will have an egalitarian society when we are able to work together on common tasks and to make decisions together.

Fraternity

'Fellowship is life', said William Morris, 'and lack of fellowship is death'. 'Fraternity', however, is the least defined of the values of the Left, whereas a huge literature exists on 'liberty' and 'equality'. Nothing is decided by arbitrary definitions. Rather let us simply ask 'when do we find what we ordinarily call fraternal behaviour?' Surely it is when we are performing some common task, work or even a team game, which we agree needs doing and is done in such a way that each of us has something to contribute? A group of men and women who want to get the job done in time and in the right way, a football team, a committee room on election day, a good committee, an army with high morale in battle, a nation at war, all these furnish examples of situations in which fraternity is not merely helpful but which positively generate fraternity. Note that fraternity does not always involve liberty — it can, better that it does; but fraternity can exist under coercion as well as voluntarily.

So it would appear, firstly, that fraternity is an attitude of mind, and one associated with activity. Fraternity is not radiating an abstract love of humanity: it arises from people actually working together towards common ends. For instance, I am doubtful how much it means for me to say that I feel fraternity towards 'Prods' or 'Taigs', blacks or whites, unless I actually work or mix with them. We may love each of these (in a rather abstract sense), respect them or simply tolerate them; we can even treat them as equals (insofar as we have occasion to be with them at all); but fraternity must at least involve working on common tasks together or in living together (like brothers in a family, with their jealousies and independence as well as bonds of circumstance and affection).

The metaphor of brotherhood needs exploring. Actual brotherhood is commonly an odd mixture of affection and rivalry, even jealousy; so fraternity does not necessarily involve men and women being literally equal, still less treating everyone the same. Perhaps, indeed, fraternity is closer to friendship than to love. Friendship is not a total identification with another and it is rarely, if ever, consistent with trying to make another over into some other image than their own — whether the image of an ideology, the image of God or one's own. Fraternity must surely accept all people, even friends, as they are — warts and all. By all means seek to involve them in common tasks; and to influence them; but then seek neither to condemn their inadequacy, nor be jealous of their superiority, nor avoid being influenced ourselves. If we are to experience genuine fraternity we must take each other as we find each other, not in fancy dress or seen through tinted glasses. We cannot say that there can be no genuine fraternity until the classless society or until we are 'born again' into some future state. Fraternity like friendship implies present simplicity and lack of ostentation and pomposity, but some restraints nonetheless, for we are dealing with other people. There is a difference between accepting the invitation to 'make yourself at home' in a friend's house, and acting 'as if it belonged to you'. Similarly if fraternity is treating people equally, this does not mean that one treats everyone as if they were, in all relevant respects, the same. W.G. Runciman's distinction is relevant, between 'equality of respect', which should be universal, and 'equality of praise', which becomes empty if universalized; people do have different talents and aptitudes which should be recognized. The only limitation on praise and reward is that no talents or aptitudes can justify social hierarchy. To a brother or sister I must be neither servile and acquiescent nor censorious and condescending.

So fraternity must involve, firstly, common tasks and activities, and secondly an exultant recognition of diversity of character. Fraternity implies individuality, not sameness; but, of course, like socialist ethics in general, it is also concerned with how individuals can work together and contribute best to the common tasks of a reforming society, living in and creating actual communities. 'From each according to his abilities, to each according to his needs.' But can fraternity cut across class lines? Is fraternity compatible with inequality?

The harsh and deromanticizing answer is, 'sometimes'. Fraternity can — for a moment — cut across the most rigid class lines. This is the fraternity engendered on great occasions, be they wars, battles, long marches, last stands or even Labour Party annual conferences. The fraternity of great occasions, of Struggle and Challenge, is, however, inherently temporary — unless the pressure is artificially kept up, as when Trotsky advocated 'permanent revolution' to ensure the monopoly of power of the Communist Party (in the right hands) and Chairman Mao argued, even as Machiavelli and Jefferson had done, that every generation must experience the intense comradeship of revolutionary renewal. Sometimes a kind of fraternity is engendered in new nations between the leader and the masses which is real and elevating for a while, but which if continued indefinitely becomes a deliberate fraud: the illusion of the leader as father or as big brother which can disguise dictatorship, despotism and continuing gross inequality.

Such momentary fraternity can lead in wholly unhumanitarian directions. Erich Remarque wrote of the 'false fraternity of the trenches' in his *All Quiet on the Western Front*. For even when released from that compulsive and deadly fraternity, years later, many who had experienced it felt during the 1920s and 1930s a sense of loss, a deep psychological void in normal life — shared indeed by many who had only read about it! Some sought to fill this void from very different sources, including both the Communist Party and the Fascist movements. The Fascists of the 1920s and 1930s tried, even short of war, to recreate this wartime atmosphere of 'blood brotherhood' or false fraternity. A once-famous book by an apostate Nazi, Von Rauschning, *The Revolution of Nihilism*, argued the paradox that people did not first march with the Nazis because they agreed with them and shared their values, but they marched because they *wanted* to gain a feeling of brotherhood and wanted to agree with them. Camping, drilling, marching, demonstrating, rioting — and beating up Jews or Communists together — gave them the experience of fraternity they desired so much. They did it for that reason.

Such fraternity of even good great occasions is not what democratic socialists want; nor one that could not apply to *any* group of human beings, irrespective of class, race, sex, nationality, religion or intelligence: we want a fraternity for all seasons and possible for all of us, self-willed and enduring. Fraternity without liberty is a nightmare, liberty without fraternity is competitive cruelty, but fraternity with liberty is humanity's greatest dream. But if fraternity is hard to find in liberal contexts, small wonder that some people may seek it in violent actions.

In modern society, fraternity is too often only experienced in civic emergencies or in the privacy of social or sporting clubs. It would be idle to pretend that those who are ordinarily able to purchase what they want (and constantly to invent new wants) are likely to feel any real sense of brotherhood with those who have to struggle all the time, and often fail, to purchase what they minimally need. Rather than brotherhood, the favoured ones are more apt to perceive threat from the disadvantaged — I could sometimes wish with more reason. Any abstract fraternity they might feel is empty of real content while their lives do not touch, while their sons and daughters so rarely intermingle and seldom marry outside their social class. Their ordinary relationships with each other are guided by the social distance arising from exploitation and work, command and obedience. The upper classes (while often indeed 'fraternal' among themselves) call for sacrifice and belt-tightening from ordinary wage-earners, but not from themselves. They admit the working classes to be patriotic insofar as they act 'responsibly', especially in matters of wage restraint, and when the unemployed do not kick back. They approach the working classes in times of crisis with the coarse, temporary affability of Shakespeare's Henry V speaking to the common soldiers on the eve of Agincourt:

> For he today who sheds his blood with me
> Shall be my brother; be he ne'er so vile
> This day shall gentle his condition.

However, there are some contrary signs of hope. While sociologists point to a declining sense of fraternity and mutual aid in traditional working classes (which is itself a relative and not irreversible matter, especially as the lesson of hard times begins to sink in), others point to an increased fraternity in the younger generation. Despite the class bias of higher education, for instance, most students for over a generation have acted in a more classless manner, in their dress, speech, life-style generally and patterns of friendship. Many try valiantly, a few successfully, to sustain this even in the world of commercial and industrial work. And they see themselves as part of a wider youth culture, heavily working class in its origins, whose music and dress may not have universal appeal, and may indeed be subject of commercial exploitation, but which is nonetheless egalitarian in spirit. This 'youth culture' has now spread throughout the Western world, tries hard to make links with the Third World consciousness, however artificial, absurd and tentative these links at times may be; and it even penetrates Eastern Europe and is a cause for worry in the Kremlin itself. All this has happened without any conscious government policy, often in the teeth of ruling classes and educational authorities: almost everywhere schooling, for instance, is less dragooned and more informal — even in the private sector that tries so hard to resist it and maintain 'Victorian values' and a proper sense of hierarchy. It need only be given a political purpose.

Contemporary women's movements are especially rich in 'fraternity'. The incongruity of the word in this context should indeed make one pause. I myself do not believe that a sensitive use of an historically male-dominated language is necessarily 'sexist', in the sense of artifically preserving male dominance. Certainly languages are hard to control. Some might argue that the very use of 'fraternity' helps perpetuate assumptions that male dominance is natural. It could. Personally I rejoice in how much fraternity at its best is exemplified in women's groups working together for common purposes as equals. But I grant two things to those who have more than nominal worries. The one is that the Fascist perversion of fraternity, the aggressive brothers' band, is indeed a strongly male image, is in many ways a revealing caricature of psychological stereotypes of manliness: aggression, competitiveness and xenophobia. The other worry is that 'sisterhood' in some ways is truly a less ambiguous image of what I am trying to convey by 'fraternity'. Think simply of any group of women spontaneously 'rallying round' to help and support another in need or trouble. 'Sisterhood' then has all the connotations of support, care, practicality, grace, sensitivity and empathy needed for the best definitions of politically minded socialists working together. In principle it would be no more strange for men to say 'liberty, equality and sisterhood' than for women to say 'liberty, equality and fraternity'. Indeed it might be salutary, for 'sisterhood' makes a clear moral point: the concept would then be liberated, indeed, from its less happy associations with 'a brothers' band against the world' or the slaughter-house ethic of the Nordic Sagas and of Sci-Fi Galactic wars rather than with good human groups able to relate peaceably as equals to all others. The words 'Peace Women', for instance, may perpetuate a sexual stereotype, but if so then it is a powerful and good one. In terms of sheer comprehensibility, however, it still seems to me, on balance, more sensible to try to desex, even to feminize, old 'fraternity', rather than to pause to rewrite most languages or to impede them with more neologisms. Thus I repeat (but with this important qualification) that amid the anti-fraternal competitiveness of capitalist society, women's groups are especially rich in counter-examples of 'fraternity', truly conceived.

Again those who talk as liberals and Social Democrats do of the need for more worker participation in industry and 'co-ownership', and those who talk as democratic socialists do of the need for industrial democracy or cooperative ownership of industry, have in common a sense that there is a vast energy and know-how ready to be released if the men and women who do the hard work could influence or control the work. And in Great Britain the 'old Tories' or true conservatives in the

Conservative Party have a sense at least of the need to preserve communities and community values, unlike the 'market liberals' in their party who seem willing to see communities disintegrate in favour of a model of a purely individualistic, competitive and careerist society. The capitalist system, however, never fully succeeded in destroying the fraternal institutions of working class life. The task of good government is to create a sense of common purpose and problems that must be solved together: fundamental economic and social policies which actually need widespread support to work for the overriding purpose of creating greater equality and a genuine, active liberty or common citizenship for all in each country and gradually for all mankind.

If more genuine fraternity or sisterhood existed, worries about literal equality and marginal differentials could be less acute. Literal equality would not guarantee fraternity unless there was also a sense of common purpose; and existing degrees of inequality must make fraternity in everyday life excessively difficult. The Duke and the dustman, the dictator and the poor peasant, may indeed feel themselves to be members of the one nation, but that nation then will be based on a sense of hierarchy, condescension and deference, not brotherhood; at best only a poor and dependent cousinhood. In Beethoven's *Fidelio* the King is converted to the principles of French enlightenment and suddenly proclaims: 'Let all men be my brothers'. He means well, but it is no good. The master and servant relationship is mutually corrupting. For, firstly, while there are kings, counts, dictators and millionaires, such gifts and flatteries are a sham and a deceit: power is never let go of and always returnable.

Both the Communist Party and the Fascist movements of the 1930s sensed a profound human need when they cultivated their emotions of fraternity simultaneously on a very small and local scale (the primal image of the brothers' band, organizing in shopfloor cells or in neighbourhood militias) and also on a vast scale (the Party and the Movement itself, even for a while the international movement). We do indeed need both. The experience of fraternity is learned in small groups; and learned best in small groups which fulfil a variety of roles — working, governing themselves and providing as many of their own services as they can: the image of the commune and of industrial democracy. But it must be extended to all humanity — certainly beyond the nation, otherwise the world will only see the deadly rivalry of East and West replaced by fear of war between North and South. And yet fraternity must be extended in such a way that the large scale does not obliterate the small. We do indeed need both.

Consider one example of a problem of balancing the large with the small, for the matter is not easy when brought down from principle and rhetoric to earth. In Great Britain we are now a multi-racial and multi-cultural society — whether we like it or not. And the English have always lived with Scottish, Welsh and Irish compatriots or neighbours. Few people now seem to favour complete *assimilation* of immigrants as *individuals*: that everyone should be 'English'. Most people now talk, albeit vaguely, of a pluralist society and the *integration* of different *communities*. We recognize that different cultures can live side by side. But can this be an excuse for tolerating gross inequalities between them in standard of living and life-chances? The socialist answer, indeed any humanitarian answer, is obvious. And can the good recognition of cultural diversity be an excuse for minorities sometimes to restrain their members by force, especially their women and children, from leaving their communities? This problem is more difficult. Surely no amount of communal fraternity can excuse injustices and unfreedoms in the light of general principles of human rights? It is hard to know where to draw the line in practice. But some lines must be drawn in public law, only after much debate, however, bringing these issues out in the open, neither suppressing nor denying them. We must protect greater cultural differences than we have tolerated or known in the past, but must also protect freedom, especially the possibility for individuals to move during their lifetime from one culture to another and sometimes back again. Both the nation and the new sub-cultures have to make political and social adjustments: such adjustments are only unjust if the majority use their power imperceptively and inflexibly — unpolitically. If the majority fail to conciliate the minority they may (in a narrow sense) be acting democratically, but they are storing up the kind of trouble for the future (as happened in Northern Ireland) that makes democracy unworkable.

Socialists must always remind themselves that economic

planning will never by itself create a more fraternal society. Simply arithmetical equality could conceivably create even fiercer competitiveness. We must not oversociologize. Social conditions can help or hinder but they cannot guarantee more fraternity, nor, fortunately, always destroy it — as people on strike in hard times show us. Fraternity is an ethic that can grow only if believed in freely and practised. It goes with simplicity, lack of ostentation, friendliness, helpfulness, kindliness, openness, lack of restraint between individuals, everyday life and a willingness to work together in common tasks. It doesn't only go with fierce memories of the trials and struggles of a movement's early days or with the temporary happy unison of party meetings — however long they last.

Yet fraternity does not mean no leadership: it only means no permanent class of leaders tomorrow and no *noblesse oblige* today — no condescension, no giving favours; but rather leaders receiving trust on account of peculiar skills of both empathy and action which are being used for common purposes popularly decided. Fraternity does mean creating by public policy as well as by individual example common purposes and cooperation in both working life and leisure. A fraternal society would be one in which there would be far more popular participation in deciding how decisions are to be made. Fraternity is frustrated by any gross inequalities of income and by the acquired and encouraged acquisitiveness of capitalism: 'the rage for the accumulation of things', as Orwell once remarked, a rage that is so obviously never satisfied and which thinks that it can only be satisfied by the exclusion of others.

Individualism

Nor is fraternity, like the socialist views of positive freedom, necessarily incompatible with individualism, unless brothers simply push too hard — this needs to be said for it worries so many people. There is individualism true and false, sociable and anti-social. If, of course, one punches into the concept of an 'individual' all that Professor Hayek does in his *Road to Serfdom, Individualism and Economic Order* and many other works (to put it briefly, the whole *laisser-faire* economic theory), then plainly man as such a programmed predator has very little interest in being fraternal. Hayekian man will obey the law only out of utilitarian self-interest; and that civil law is not able, though it may rashly try, to change the natural 'laws of economics'. But more humane concepts of 'the individual' should raise no problems for socialists or others. All we need to say is, anthropologically, that mankind is unique and that one aspect of that uniqueness is that each member of the species is unique; and, philosophically, that every man must be treated as an end in himself, never as a means to an end. Having said this, there is no greater reason in principle why human beings should not act with fraternity towards each other rather than with aversion, with cooperativeness rather than aggression or competition. Both images are induced cultural achievements and owe more to nurture than to nature.

Socialism does, however, have a distinctive modulation of this general view of *homo sapiens*. Socialists, after all, stress sociability. Some, like Kropotkin and the anarchists, benignly 'cheat' by building into their model of human nature a cooperative spirit of mutual aid, just as some social biologists will picture natural man as 'red in tooth and claw', or at least a little Reaganite. Stressing sociability as a cultural achievement, some socialists go overboard in seeing social classes as more real than individuals; so that, once again, true individualism can only exist after that mythic, almost eschatological event, the Revolution. There is no need to go that far. Some suggest, for instance, that it is better to talk of individual human *identity* rather than conservative 'character', Marxist 'class identity' or Rousseauistic 'personality'. Many people today take for granted that the main object of 'a liberal education' and of personal life is to develop something called 'personality' and to attain 'self-knowledge'. 'Personality' implies that I am myself at my best when I am performing spontaneous, unique and 'authentic' acts (all over the place). Many libertarian socialists hold this view, but it is a view hard to reconcile with the socialist stress on sociability and cooperation: 'personalities' are all very well when they challenge established conventions; they are less helpful in creating new conventions of social justice and a fraternity for all seasons.

My 'identity', however, implies something both individual and social. It is individual because it is uniquely mine, but what it actually consists of is a series of mutual recognitions with other people in a social context. It is no use my believing that I have a true but suppressed personality unless I can show some signs of it recognizable and tolerable to other people. And you cannot expect me to take to you as a person unless you present some attributes recognizable and tolerable to me. And each in trying to gain recognition for a 'personality' may end up with a tolerably civilized 'identity'. Thus individualism should be limited by deliberate sociability. This is far from an abstract or empty remark, as two very different examples may show. I think that I have no right to take heavy drugs (and that you have a duty to stop me), both because of the social consequences involved (for even if you do not presume to try to coerce and cure, someone will have to pick up and throw away the desocialized pieces), and also because I will destroy my sociability, certainly that adaptability and flexibility that enables a self to relate to other selves in the real world. Also I would not really like to become suddenly very rich; for even if it was not obviously at the expense of others (like winning the pools), it would threaten my existing relationships and therefore identity — with which I am not entirely unhappy, at least have learned to live with once I gave up the adolescent habit of asking, like poor Peer Gynt, 'who am I really?' Of course extreme poverty is more obviously damaging to personal identity and the more widespread problem. There are more Woyzecks than Gynts.

Democratic socialists, unlike some old Marxists, must allow that sociability is a wider concept than social class. Class, in a class society, is inevitably a very important part of identity, but it can never be a sufficient account of individual identity. To be more formal and theoretical, the concept of social class works well with many aggregate predictions of behaviour, but less well with 'exceptions' of individual behaviour, which are often so important both politically, intellectually and morally. Individuals should cultivate both fraternity and tolerance as they try by collective action to move towards an egalitarian and libertarian society.

Yet move how fast?

'Eternity', said William Blake, 'is in love with the products of time.' When an evolutionary transformation is attempted in countries with long established representative institutions, many conventions are a brake upon progress: but the price of trying to ignore such brakes, experience suggests, is simply too great. When a revolution (as an event) occurs in countries which have not had such a tradition, it is desperately difficult for those in power to see the need to create genuine representative institutions, if they even appear to impede the speed of social advance. But such is life, or rather society. Yet in neither condition is democratic socialism impossible. Perhaps some Marxists truly believe that liberty fatally obstructs progress and that parliamentary institutions are incompatible with socialism; but the reaction of the Russian leaders to Czechoslovakia in 1968 and to Poland in 1981 did not follow from such theoretical considerations: theirs was the sadly normal reaction of any autocracy faced by popular challenge.

Any consideration of the time-scales involved in industrialization in Western Europe, or of the bad consequences of an imposed, rapid industrialism from the top, whether on the Stalinist model in Russia or on the Meiji model in Japan, must convince socialists and their opponents alike that the enterprise is a long and difficult one. Even after violent revolutions, old attitudes survive to an astonishing extent; it is as misleading to underestimate the changes in post-revolutionary Russia, indeed, as it is to ignore continuities. And from a base-camp established amid representative or parliamentary institutions, the time needed for the establishment of a socialist society may appear desperately long. But the built-in political necessity of any British socialist government having to carry with them an enfranchised public opinion, as well as an already organized trade union movement (including both civil servants and teachers), guarantees that each move of the camp further and further up the mountain will be built upon solid ground, less likely to slip backwards or simply to get stuck.

Serious socialist leaders should not give hostages to fortune by promising more than they can fulfil in the short term. The *short term* is the life of a Parliament and is the period of building a base and support for social change. Short-term legislative measures must respond to immediate problems and be popular or at least widely acceptable in the country at large (especially if they need a response in the behaviour of working people to work at all, as so much economic and social legislation does). But short-term measures should be consistent with middle-term theories about *how* to achieve long-term goals, such as an egalitarian society; or at the very least, amid the often desperate contingencies of politics and economic events, not inconsistent with those goals.

The *middle-period* is the period of trying to change attitudes and values, both by persuasion or by the removal of institutions whose main function is to maintain privilege and social stratification, be it private education, private medicine or the investment policies of banks and pension funds. Even the removal of some of these institutions is unlikely to work in a socialist direction if not done gradually, or unless enough of the people who work them are at least willing to serve the new system unobstructively. In retrospect it does not seem to have been a very bright idea of the Labour Government of 1945–50 simply to replace the management of so much industry by civil servants, without the generation of socialist managers and engineers that was by then the forgotten part of the great vision of Shaw, Wells and the Webbs, the role they cast for the new polytechnic institutions. Middle-period planning and transition plainly requires at least a generation simply because of the need for attitudinal change: it is not possible in the life of any one or two Parliaments.

Yet amid short-term legislation, middle-period strategies have to be canvassed. People have to be convinced of and made familiar with the new ideas. Educational change has to be undertaken in the short-term programme to provide the personnel and the skills for the strategy of the middle-term structural changes. But such changes and the strategies themselves have to be debated, speculated about, before they can be established. And all the time the *long-term* values of the classless society are to be asserted and refined: what will the social differences of the sexes be, or the role of cultural minorities in a classless society? A socialist movement needs moral philosophers as well as economists, or rather needs to popularize both modes of discourse in a speculative, not a dogmatic spirit. Again, 'the ethically desirable must be the sociologically possible'. The bounds of present possibilities can be extended, but only over time and by debate, not edict.

For a socialist movement simply to campaign on long-term values would be absurd. For it simply to campaign on immediate reforms of the present system is, indeed, not socialist at all (simply desperate patchwork on a worn-out garment). It needs always to campaign on three different levels: (i) short-term tactical reforms within the system to build a basis of popular confidence for advance; (ii) middle-term strategies to change the system; and (iii) long-term persuasion to work a new system in a new spirit. These levels do not contradict, they complement each other so long as the distinctions about time are made clear. Politicians are pretty useless who can only dwell in one dimension; public servants may have to. Party manifestos would look very different if written in this manner (more socialist and less Chartist). But even if it may be a long time before institutions will exhibit socialist values, socialists can. Part of persuasion is reasoning but part is example.

Government must work through stages, but individuals can simultaneously work amid short-term limitations, plan for middle-term change and speculate on the future, without hypocrisy or self-deceit. Young civil servants or managers are not 'selling out to the system' if they implement policies which they think are mistaken or work within institutions they think to be regressive, so long as their criticisms are made and heard within or without the workplace. They *can* help change the climate of expectation and should hope to use their knowledge, and expect to be consulted, in formulating middle-term strategies. Social workers are not 'shoring up the system' if they help real people in trouble: they are helping people in trouble. With socialist policies they may be able to tackle problems in better ways, they may have less problems, but they must convince not desert their clients. Teachers are not betraying children by teaching our bad syllabuses well, so long as they use every opportunity they have in the present system to change them or at least to refuse to moralize them. If socialist policies and greater social equality diminish both the feeling of hopelessness and the class-labels of learning, however, there may be greater motivation, more learning and less teaching. Factory workers are not working for capitalism, they are working for a living wage. But with socialist policies wage differentials could count for less and their skills could be used to better effect. It is not romantic in the least to think that 'industrial democracy' could be more efficient than private ownership; it is a serious hypothesis to be tested and assessed in many different ways, in firms of different size and on different time-scales. Working 'within the system', efficiency has to be proved, but in being proved the assumptions of our existing definitions of 'efficiency' can be challenged: is capital-intensive machinery really less costly than labour-intensive processes of work in all conditions? Someone has to pick up the bill or pay the cost of labour-saving that becomes unemployment.

As well as the classes, there are the sexes. A woman is not necessarily selling the pass to prove herself as good as a man in a man's world, not unless she rests content with achievement and fails to use her position to try to change the assumptions of that world. Women today are less and less content to work for men in the home; they too work for wages because they need to, or even when middle class women do not need to, they then work to prove their independence and equality. Expectations of radical change already exist, and need but to be built upon. Pressure groups have modified both public policy and public opinion even within our present society. Some women may not have to wait for the classless society to act like equals and to be treated as equals. But equality of the sexes without social equality will be hamstrung by class differences and opportunities. Progressive middle class women should beware of imposing their values on working class women. They campaign, to take an example important for women, against the impersonal regime of hospitals and to have their babies 'at home'. Being individualistic, they do not like being bullied and categorized in hospitals; and middle class women are also, on average, healthier, so less at risk outside hospital. But they should not make a cult of home-birth and imply that other women are unnatural not to do so, until such time as bad housing conditions and poverty no longer make infant mortality so dramatically different between the social classes. We live side by side but in different time-scales, even biologically and demographically. But middle class women should not be ashamed of making differential advances to equality in education and employment, for instance: such example is likely to spread, in time. Yet advanced feminists should be aware of how small a minority they are; and that to capture a London Borough or even a Labour Party Conference is far from conquering the country.

Advance must be by 'small steps', indeed; but steps if they are really steps should have high rises as well as broad treads, and need to be placed on top of each other, not scattered surrealistically over the landscape as opportunity knocks or according to who holds what Ministry. I like the metaphor of rapid small steps rather than few giant steps. Nonetheless in both short-term and middle-period planning, differential advance can be made. The idea that societies are systems is a highly abstract one and should not be applied too literally to limit practice. 'The whole man moves at once', as Hoff-mansthal was wont to quote, but societies are not like that — only in the imagination of Engels and Hayek. Every plan must be flexible enough to allow unexpected opportunities to be seized on one part of the line, costly attacks abandoned for the moment at another, so long as there is a general move forward.

Socialist movements in the West were in danger of losing confidence in their leaders' wills or abilities to move towards a classless and more free society. The rank-and-file party activists are often grossly unrealistic, often in too much of a hurry (and anything of this kind made in a hurry is not likely to last); but if they are it is at least in part the fault of past leaders. They were so pragmatic that they both lost sight of and could never talk with conviction about either middle-term restruc-turing of institutions or long-term realisation of socialist values.

The ways and means towards a democratic and participatory egalitarian society must be debated again, and in concrete terms: old Fabian precision animated and humanized by a broader moral perspective and a greater toleration for those particular and varying inequalities which arise from conscious decisions by groups of equals, not from the permanent domi-nance of social class. 'Working together' should be the slogan, not 'Doing good'.

So we have to learn to think in terms of different time-scales (not wings or factions) simultaneously. They do not contra-dict, they complement each other and politicians are useless who live in one dimension alone. We have to react to day-to-day events realistically and pragmatically, respecting people's opinions as they are — but not mere pragmatism. We also have to pursue middle-term policy for the eradication of poverty and other injustices — consistently, which means winning elections and changing opinion slowly, as well as determining long-term priorities. And socialists have all the time to practise a code of morality based on fraternity which we can believe will be natural to all in the long-term future condition of an egalitarian society in which all men are free — in the present world so few are genuinely free. Socialists must not treat other people as if they are already living in the future; to do so is fantasy or oppression. But socialists themselves must be a testimony that some better, more fraternal and cooperative type of human relations is possible. Otherwise what does it matter who can manage the declining economy best?

$$*\qquad*\qquad*$$

Perhaps all this has fallen between advocacy and defence, too philosophical for some and not philosophical enough for others. I believe that socialism must be able to present its theories and its doctrines, as well as its campaign policies, in a simple language of common sense and common understanding. But, nonetheless, it is not easy to fight on three fronts simultaneously: against socialists impatient of political means; against pragmatists who think that benign public administration is all we need or can have; and against sceptics who think that all socialism is inherently anti-political and anti-libertarian and who themselves believe that social hierarchy, poverty and unemployment are the prices that all must pay for the culture and liberties of some. But it must be done, and in the long run all people will want to be citizens and citizenship cannot be fully practised other than among equals.

And in the short run, a socialist society is not attainable; but we can lead our lives in an egalitarian and fraternal manner. Example can be as effective and persuasive as legislation in shaping a better future.

Bibliography

Here is neither a full list of my sources nor a scholarly bibliography, rather some books which I find interesting and helpful and are accessible to the ordinary reader — thus I have ignored the vast internalized and narcissistic Marxiological literature of the now rapidly ageing 'New Left'.

History of Socialism

G.D.H. Cole, *History of Socialism*, 5 vols (Macmillan, London, 1953-60) is still unrivalled for it's scope and it's lively biographical treatment, so easy to skip and dip. It largely replaced Max Beer's *A General History of Socialism and Social Struggles*, 5 vols (Leonard Parsons, London, 1922-25, translated by H.J. Stenning), except that Beer has far more on precursors and on social movements, and is far better on German sources. David Caute, *The Left in Europe Since 1789* (Weidenfeld, London, 1966) is short, popular, illustrated but sound. A wide-ranging and enthusiastic anthology is Christopher Hampton, ed., *A Radical Reader: the struggle for change in England* (Penguin, Harmondsworth, 1984).

Marx and Marxism

D. McLellan, ed., *Karl Marx: Selected Writings* (OUP, Oxford, 1977) is a well balanced anthology of his thought, whereas Eugene Kamenka, ed., *The Portable Karl Marx* (Penguin, Harmondsworth, 1983) has more on his life, and is more defensive. How Marx was used by the international Communist movement in its heyday can be seen in Emile Burns, ed., *A Handbook of Marxism* (Gollancz, London, 1935).

Isaiah Berlin, *Karl Marx: His Life and Environment* (Home University Library, Oxford, 1948) is not favoured by Marxists but is concise and judicious as well as trenchant, only rivalled, with even greater brevity, by David McLellan, *Marx* (Fontana, London, 1975) or at greater length by his *Karl Marx: His Life and Thought* (Macmillan, London, 1973). Harold Laski's Introduction to the Labour Party's centenary edition of *The Communist Manifesto* (Allen & Unwin, London, 1948) is an excellent account of the manifesto's context and influence. Jon Elster, *Making Sense of Marx* (CUP, Cambridge, 1985) is heavy-going without some academic philosophy but is the most rigorous and successful attempt yet to sort out great sense from great verbiage and what is alive and what is dead in Marx himself.

   See also on Marx, George Lichtheim, *Marxism: An Historical and Critical Study* (Routledge, London, 1961); Perry Anderson, *Considerations on Western Marxism* (New Left Books, London, 1976) and his *In the Tracts of Historical Materialism*; T. Bottomore, *Sociology and Socialism* (Wheatsheaf, Brighton, 1984); and Thomas Sowell, *Marxism, Philosophy and Economics* (Allen & Unwin, London, 1985). And on the aftermath three first-hand accounts, John Reed, *Ten Days That Shook the World* (Penguin, Harmondsworth, 1966); Eugene Lyons; *Assignment Utopia* (Harrap, London, 1938); Victor Serge, *Memoirs of a Revolutionary* (OUP, London, 1967); and three critical analyses, Isaac Deutscher, *Stalin: a political biography* (OUP, London, 1949); A.J. Polan, *Lenin and the End of Politics* (Methuen, London, 1984); and David Caute's *The Fellow Travellers* (Weidenfeld, London, 1973) is an antidote to romanticising the old international Communist movement.

   Leszek Kolakowski's *Main Currents of Marxism*, vol. 1, *The Founders*, vol. 2, *The Golden Age* and vol. 3, *The Breakdown* (Clarendon Press, Oxford, 1978), translated from the Polish by P.S. Falla, is in a class of it's own: a masterpiece both of history and critical analysis.

British Democratic Socialist Tradition

A short but excellent anthology is Anthony Wright, ed., *British Socialism: socialist thought from the 1880s to 1960s* (Methuen, London, 1983), and good and up-to-date is Geoffrey Foote, *The Labour Party's Political Thought: a History* (Croom Helm, London, 1985), as is Kenneth O. Morgan, *Labour People: Leaders and Lieutenants, Hardie to Kinnock* (OUP, Oxford, 1987). For the early history of British socialism, Max Beer's *A History of British Socialism*, 2 vols (1919), has been reprinted in a one volume illustrated edition with introductions by R.H. Tawney and by Ken Coates (Spokesman, Nottingham, 1984). Stanley Pierson, *British Socialists: the Journey from Fantasy to Politics* (Harvard University Press, London, 1979), shows how the ideas associated with the Labour Party emerged from sects around the turn of last century, and the story continues in Norman and Jeanne Mackenzie, *The First Fabians* (Quartet, London, 1979), J.M. Winter, *Socialism and the Challenge of War: ... 1912–18* (Routledge, London, 1974), and Ross Terrill's *R.H. Tawney and His Times: Socialism and Fellowship* (Andre Deutsch, London, 1974).

Among classic and influential writings were: *Fabian Essays* (Fabian Society, London, 1889); Sidney Webb, *Socialism in England* (Sonnenschein, London, 1890); Sidney and Beatrice Webb, *A Constitution for the Socialist Commonwealth of Great Britain* (Longmans, London, 1920); H.G. Wells, *This Misery of Boots* (Fabian Society, London, 1907); George Bernard Shaw, *The Intelligent Woman's Guide to Socialism and Capitalism* (Constable, London, 1928); Robert Blatchford, *Merrie England* (Clarion Press, London, 1908); J. Ramsey MacDonald, *The Socialist Movement* (Home University Library, London, 1911); G.D.H. Cole, *Self-Government in Industry* (Bell, London, 1917); R.H. Tawney, *The Acquisitive Society* (Bell, London, 1921 and Collins, 1961) and his *Equality* (1935) with a new introduction by Richard Titmuss (Allen & Unwin, London, 1964); Harold Laski, *A Grammar of Politics*, 5th ed. (Allen & Unwin, London 1948); Evan Durbin, *The Politics of Democratic Socialism* (Routledge, London, 1940); and George Orwell: *The Lion and the Unicorn: Socialism and the English Genius* (Secker & Warburg, London, 1941 and Penguin, 1982).

After the deaths of Laski, Tawney and Cole there was a long dearth of thinking, all seemed either Marxism or mere pragmatism, except for Richard Titmus, *The Irresponsible Society* (Fabian Society, London, 1960) and C.R.S. Crosland, *The Future of Socialism* (Cape, London, 1956).

The Revival of British Democratic Socialist Thought

The Labour Party's defeat of 1979 and the ideological intensity of Thatcherite conservatism (more correctly neo-liberalism) has prompted a remarkable literature, some by Marxists or ex-Marxists coming back to earth but also none Marxists trying to revive and modernize the old democratic socialist principles and theories: Evan Luard, *Socialism Without the State* (Macmillan, London, 1979); E.P. Thompson, *Writing By Candlelight* (Merlin, London, 1980); Eric Hobsbawm's essay 'The Forward March of Labour Halted?' reprinted in a book of that same title edited by M. Jacques and F. Mulhern (Verso, London, 1981); Geoff Hodgson, *Labour at the Crossroads* (Martin Robertson, Oxford, 1981); Michael Foot, *My Kind of Socialism* (an *Observer* reprint, Jan. 1982); Julian Le Grand, *The Strategy of Equality* (Allen & Unwin, London, 1982); Gavin Kitching, *Rethinking Socialism* (Methuen, London, 1983); Alec Nove, *The Economics of Feasible Socialism* (Allen & Unwin, London, 1983); Raymond Plant, *Equality, Markets and the State* (Fabian Society, London, Tract 494, 1984); Bernard Crick, *Socialist Values and Time* (Fabian Society, London, Tract 495, 1984); Mike Rustin, *For Pluralist Socialism* (Verso, London, 1985);

Bryan Gould, *Socialism and Freedom* (Macmillan, London, 1985); Antony Wright, *Socialism: Theory and Practices* (Oxford University Press, 1986); Neil Kinnock, *The Future of Socialism* (Fabian Society, London, Tract 509, 1986; and Roy Hattersley, *Choose Freedom: The Future for Democratic Socialism* (Michael Joseph, London, 1987); and April Carter, *The Politics of Womens Rights* (Longmans, London, 1987).

Index

Acton, John Emerich
  Edward Dalberg,
  Lord, 20–1
anarchism, 25, 39–41, 107
Arendt, Hannah, 26
Aristotle, 3, 7

Babeuf, Gracchus, 21
Berlin, Sir Isaiah 50–1,
  85–6
Bestor, Arthur, 37
Bevan, Aneurin, 74
'Black Report' (on
  inequalities of health),
  94–5
Blake, William, 19
Blanqui, Louis-August,
  38–9
Blatchford, Robert 69–70
Brisbane, Arthur, 37
Burke, Edmund, 19
Burns, Robert, 8–9

Carpenter, Edward, 67–8
citizenship, 2, 81–2
class, 7, 79, 92–3, 95–6
Cohn, Norman, 4
Cole, G.D.H., 29, 73
communism, see Marxism
  and socialism

Communist Manifesto,
  48–50, 54
Communist Party, 62–5
conservatism, 19, 79
cooperatives, 31, 41, 43–5
Crosland, Antony, 75–6
Crossman, R.H.S., 75
Czechoslovakia (the
  'Prague Spring'), 80

democracy, 6–7, 10, 29–30,
  74–5
doctrine, see theory

education, 7, 83, 87
egalitarianism, 1–2, 72, 76,
  88–98;
  and individualism, 89–92
  and incomes, 91–3
  and health, 95–6
Elster, John, Making Sense
  of Marx, 55–7
Enfantin, Barthelemy-
  Prosper, 34
Engels, Friedrich, 51
equality, see egalitarianism

Fabian Society, x, 73, 75,
  77, 79

fascism, 101
feminism, *see* women's
    rights
Foot, Michael, 65
Foote, Geoffrey, ix
Fourier, Charles, 29, 34–7
fraternity, 98–106;
    and community, 103–4
    and ethnicity, 105
    and fascism, 100–1, 104
    and feminism, 102–3
freedom, *see liberty*
French Revolution, *see*
    revolution

Hayek, F.A., 78
Hobbes, Thomas, 92, 96,
    98
Honderich, Ted, 95

ideology, defined, ix–x,
    57–8, 63–4
individualism, 13, 69,
    106–8
intolerance, 62–5

Kant, Immanuel, 10
Kinnock, Neil, 76–7
Kitching, Gavin, ix
Kolakowski, Leszek, 14

Labour Party, ix, 66, 76,
    80, 82–3
Laski, Harold, 71
Leninism, 60–3
liberalism, 79, 82, 94
liberty, 39–40, 62–3, 65,
    71–2, 75–6, 78, 84–8

and personality, 85
and citizenship, 86–7
and participation, 88

MacDonald, Ramsey, 70
Marx, Karl, 19, 25, 40–1,
    82, 84
    and Darwin, 51–2
    and Proudhon, 40–1, 51
    and Saint-Simon, 52
    capital accumulation, 53,
        82
    capitalism, 54–6
    class struggle, 53
    economic determinism,
        57
    materialism, 54
    moralism, 55–6
    revolution, 56–7, 59
Marxism, 47–50, 57–8, 66,
    78, 80, 82, 84; *see also*
    Leninism
Mill, John Stuart, 7, 83
Millenarianism, 4
Morris, William, 67, 98

Napoleon I, Bonaparte, 16,
    31–2
New Lanark, 42–3; *see also*
    Owen, Robert

Orwell, George, 64, 73–4,
    89, 106
Owen, Robert, 29, 42–6

phalansteres, 35–6; *see also*
    Fourier, Charles
Popper, Sir Karl, 58

poverty, 90, 92, 95–6
progress, idea of, 24–5
property, 40
Proudhon, Pierre-Joseph,
    39–42
Putney Debates, 8–9

Rawls, John, 91
Revolution, 10–11, 14–20,
    22–3, 26–7, 39, 56–7
  American, 17
  French, 14–27, 30–1
  Russian, 59–61
rhetoric, defined, ix
Rousseau, Jean-Jacques,
    10–13, 44
Runciman, W.G., 91, 97,
    99–100
Rustin, Michael, ix

Saint-Simon, Claude-Henri
    de Rouvray, Comte
    de, 29, 32–4
Serge, Victor, 62–3
Shaw, George Bernard,
    70–1
Shostakovitch, Dmitri,
    64–65
Silone, Ignazio, 64–5
sociability, 107–8; *see also*
    fraternity
socialism, defined, 3, 28–30
  and Christianity, 4–5, 9,
    74, 79
  British, 66, 70, 73–4,

76–9, 88–9
  communitarian, 36
  democratic, viii, 39, 74–5
  early, 1, 28–31
  institutions, 80–1
  primitive, 1–2
  utopian, 4, 19, 51
  see also Marxism *and*
    Stalinism
Stalinism, 62–5

Tawney, R.H., 72, 86–8,
    92
terror, 20; *see also* violence
theory, defined, ix–x, 79
time (and time-scales),
    109–14
  the short-term, 109–10
  the middle-period, 110
  the long-term, 111
Tocqueville, Alexis de, 15,
    17
tolerance, see *intolerance*
Townsend, Peter, 95
trade unions, 45–6
Trotsky, Leon, 62, 100

values, importance of, 83
violence, 26, 95–96

Webb, Beatrice, 69
Webb, Sidney, 68–9
women's rights, 1–2,
    102–3, 112
Wright, Antony, ix